CW00330390

The Science of Attraction:
What Behavioral & Evolutionary Psychology Can Teach Us About Flirting, Dating, and Mating

By Patrick King
Social Interaction and Conversation Coach at
www.PatrickKingConsulting.com

Table of Contents

Introduction

Michael is a long-time client, and when I think back to where we started, it's startling.

When we first met, he characterized himself as an introvert, although I quickly learned that his self-assessment was mostly a cover for his lack of social confidence and lack of confidence in general.

He was twenty-nine years old, had never had a girlfriend, and had never even kissed a girl. I knew something deeper than just being an introvert was holding him back. Long before we met, he had made assumptions about how to treat women, and no one had ever corrected him or showed him why those assumptions were wrong. Unfortunately those assumptions and the results he was getting only further cemented his poor opinion of himself.

With my prompting, he began to use online dating sites and dating apps. He was able to get some matches, and one of our first coaching sessions was about how to keep a conversation going with a woman—which can be nerve-wracking even for those of us who call ourselves social butterflies and natural flirts.

Michael was at a dead end and didn't know what to do. He genuinely had begun to think that there was something deeply unattractive about him. But there wasn't! Michael wasn't boring or off-putting in conversation; he just needed to learn how to structure a conversation to be more interesting. He showed me a text conversation between him and a female friend whom he was interested in—and that's when a pattern became obvious.

If his goal was to make his female friend like him in the way he wanted her to, he was accomplishing absolutely the opposite.

1. He was sending her three texts for every one she sent, and although her replies were one sentence at most, his were voluminous. If his texts had been green

and hers blue, the screen would have looked like the fairway on a golf course.

2. He was making it painfully clear that he was constantly clearing his entire schedule for her and that spending even a minute of time with her was his first, second, and third priority. He said as much explicitly and made sure to always inquire about her availability weeks in advance.

3. He was sending the text equivalent of chain email messages such as "How's your Monday going?" and "Happy hump day!" just to be able to start conversations that had died the previous day.

Michael's initial question to me was about why she seemed to be pulling away even though they had so much fun when they hung out. He really liked this girl, and was treating her with what he thought was a flattering amount of attention. What was going wrong? I had my own ideas about how those hangouts actually went and why she was getting as cold as a glacier toward him.

The answer is likely plain as day to you as well: too much, too eager, too available, all too soon.

When you smother someone, you hem in

their independence and make it seem as if you have nothing better to do with your time. You are perceived as someone with low social value and even less sexual attraction. There's no mystery or compelling reason for others to be interested in you because you've already presented them with everything they could want from you (we'll be looking at this principle in more detail later in the book).

I told him as much, and my explanation hinged on understanding people's psychology and what makes them want something. But even beyond psychology, I had to tell Michael that sex, dating, relationships . . . they were all about *attraction*. How much we attract one another boils down to the unconscious triggers that make people act one way versus another. It was logical and instinctual, but there was no hard evidence I could generally use to explain it.

You generally know the logic, but it can be difficult to articulate because your argument can also be boiled down to "Well, this is my opinion from my experiences." I had plenty of anecdotal knowledge from my own experiences and even those of other clients, but I thought there must be other things I could draw on to support my advice and opinion.

This got me thinking—I know that I have a pretty good chance of being correct when I make reads like that, but was there a way I could bolster and improve my understanding of what makes people act unconsciously? Even better, could I find peer-reviewed studies of the unconscious markers that create effective flirting, lead to sex, and emulate love?

This book takes what I have learned about human psychology and combines it with hard evidence to give you a real path toward engineering attraction and feelings of love. It takes actions you perform sometimes but don't know why and gives you a nifty guideline to follow to actually subconsciously create the effect you intend to.

Everyone likes to parade their opinion as gospel, but that's because they form their opinions based on a sample size of one—themselves. Here, let's use the data from thousands and let you date better based on facts and evidence, which actually provides an objective solution to your dating troubles.

The solution for Michael's texting woes was simpler than most because it played mostly on one pretty common psychological factor—

availability. As you'll see, there's a lot of evidence to suggest that we tend to think that people are less available have higher mater value, and are therefore more attractive.

TEXTING=
ALL
ABOUT
AVAILABILITY
DON'T
BE
AVAILABLE

My prescription for Michael was to avoid always initiating the conversation, to match the intervals of her replies, to actively spend time with other women, and to be less available when making plans with her.

Now, I get it: most situations are much more complex than this one, but when you can make something as unpredictable as emotion and attraction a little bit more predictable, it gives you a massive advantage in generating the type of attraction you've always wanted. Our focus here will not be on opinion but on taking peer-revied research and creating ways to apply their findings to our everyday life. Sometimes, the common wisdom will be vindicated, but sometimes you may be surprised that the old gender stereotypes are not always accurate or useful.

Is this book for people who are looking to increase their chances of getting the opposite sex into bed, or is it for those who value long-term relationships and marriage? Well, it's both. The reason is because both journeys usually start with that all important step:

attraction. Luckily, even though attraction seems so hard to put your finger on, the science can help us understand what actually makes us look like good potential mates— and what doesn't. My hope is that whatever your ultimate goal for yourself, you are able to use this book as part textbook and part instruction to help you build the kind of romantic connections you want.

Chapter 1. Animal Attraction

Looking at attraction through the lens of biology is actually the purest way to see it.

All the extreme trappings of the modern-day dating scene—Ferraris, tiny bikinis, sprawling mansions, pick-up lines—ultimately work toward the exact same purpose. They create attraction in an instinctual and almost animalistic way that we can't really rationalize to ourselves. They excite and release hormones, and then *something* happens. We don't know how to explain it, but we know it when we see it! It's happened for thousands of years, and only recently have we as a species been able to study scientifically what is actually happening when two people make eye contact with each other across the room or decide to move in together.

Often, we don't fully understand our own actions, but they can usually be boiled down to one of the factors presented in this chapter. This is because attraction has been hard-coded in our genes. We have evolved over thousands of years to be attracted to certain aspects and traits that indicate that someone will be a *good* partner—in biological terms, at least.

We can see this in our conscious actions: in the beginning phases of dating someone new, you do this to an incredible degree. You pay for everything, you put your best face and outfit on, you act courteously, and you generally try to make your best impression. You make sure you smell nice and look good and pay special attention to showcasing your talents and skills. We present all our positives while subtly obscuring our negative traits and shortcomings. This influences everything from haircuts to wearing high-heeled shoes.

How do we recognize these effects in our subconscious actions? Well, some of the aforementioned *conscious* actions are *subconscious* to some! Just because something seems like a no-brainer in terms of attracting a mate doesn't mean it's a no-brainer to everyone. Why do men suddenly suck in their guts and puff out their chest when a beautiful woman enters the room, and why do women flip their hair and also puff out their chests when a handsome man walks in? If someone doesn't realize they are doing that by instinct, imagine how many of our actions or criteria for mates we are simply using by unexamined reflex?

The point is, our ways of generating attraction are mostly subconscious and mostly biological and evolutionary by nature. Even the way you talk to the opposite sex and attempt to flirt has biological roots and is not a product of random chance. It explains why you tend to be attracted to certain types of people and even why certain types repulse you.

At the most basic level, this is best summed up with the *sociobiological theory of attraction*, which puts everything through the perspective of propagating our offspring (that's the biology part) in our particular society (that's the sociological part). In other words, what heavily influences attractiveness in each gender is an unconscious consideration of the likelihood of children and genetic offspring.

Men will seek young, attractive women—

women who can physically bear children and aren't sexually involved with others so as to reduce the chance of raising another male's children. Women will seek men not necessarily based on physical strength, but rather on power and dominance within a society. They are seeking to provide safety and security for their children, and that can be found in many forms. You can already see how this theory plays out in our modern era.

PROVIDER BUT ALSO PROTECTOR

You can see the common stereotypes of men being more physically shallow, while women are more financially shallow. Could it actually be true, for non-nefarious, subconscious biological reasons? Some would say yes. Human beings are powerfully influenced by our biology, but we are also a complex species. What about the seventy-year-old couple who claim to be more madly in love with one another than ever before, even though both are retired, have no financial worries and have long since forgotten about child rearing? What about young women who get obsessed with men who are neither physically attractive nor financially successful? And no matter how raging any teenager's libido is, they are also a demographic known for strenuously *avoiding* pregnancy!

All this is to say that though biology is a significant influence on human sexuality (biology), it's not the only one (culture). Nevertheless, by understanding one of the oldest and most fundamental aspects of human attraction, we start to see that attraction is not quite as mysterious and unpredictable as we may have thought.

The Neurochemistry of Attraction

Using neuroimaging techniques like MRIs, scientists have been able to observe the physiological changes in the brain that happen when people fall in love, or even when they think about someone they're attracted to. Certain brain structures show increased activity—and certain parts nearly switch off.

One part that shows reduced activity is the frontal cortex. This is the area of the brain responsible for judgment, self-control and higher order cognition. Semir Zeki at the University College London explains how a team of researchers asked people to look at pictures of those they were in love with, then watched what happened in their brains. With the judgment parts of the brain shut down, it's as though criticism and doubt are momentarily suspended—it's the

19

neurological equivalent of rose-tinted glasses. This may have an important evolutionary function, since being a bit more forgiving in our appraisals of the opposite sex makes bonding and reproduction more likely.

Another area of the brain that shuts down is one associated with fear and negative emotions. This makes sense, since if people are unable to overcome this hesitation, they'll never be brave enough to approach others and risk the perils of romantic attachment. If you've ever seen a friend totally besotted with a new partner (or you have been in this position yourself!), you'll know that love and attraction can make people fearless and even reckless, completely unconcerned with the consequences of their actions as they fall head over heels.

SHE MUST FEEL NO FEAR. CALM HER

The neurological picture of attraction and love confirms what many people have long suspected: that love is irrational, uncontrollable, and not in the least predictable. That, in fact, we "lose our minds" and in a very real sense stop being able to think critically about things. While the poets are sure something mystical is happening, the evolutionary biologist might point to the fact that when it comes to attraction and mating, the higher brain is simply not a part of the picture!

What does this mean for anyone wanting to increase their attractiveness and make those connections with others? Well, hopefully you can see it has nothing to do with saying the right words or ticking the right boxes. It's not possible to have a reasoned, logical argument with someone and *convince* them to find you attractive. And people aren't attracted just because they decide they want to be. Rather, initial sexual attraction is a purely biological, unconscious and embodied phenomenon.

Humans evolved from animals who did not possess the higher cortical brain structures we possess now and so didn't use language or reason or critical thinking. But just because humans now have the ability to think, plan, imagine, analyze, and create, it doesn't mean we've lost our animal origins—in fact, the realm of dating, sex, and relationships may be where our more primal biology becomes most obvious. Whether you are looking for a quick fling or a long term, committed, and loving relationship, the fact is that most connections begin with at least a flicker of animal attraction.

Let's apply this:

The attracted, in-love brain is one where fear and hesitation are at an all-time low, and so are rationality, doubt and analytical thinking. If you hope to inspire loved up feelings in someone else, you need to understand that attraction cannot exist in a fearful mind, or one that is caught up in analytical rumination—that applies to you and to the person you'd like to attract!

Before we dive into the different approaches and principles of building attraction, we start with these fundamentals:

- Attraction can never build if we are inducing fear, hesitation, panic, or worry in other people. Likewise, we will seldom inspire others to be attracted to us if we are acting from a place of fear and nervousness. One of the best things you can do for your dating game? Relax. *Genuinely* relax. In the same way, keep in mind that you never want to pressure anyone or make them feel awkward, unrelaxed, hurried, or as though you are forcing something. They need to feel relaxed, too.
  Attraction flourishes when we switch off the analytical logical mind. Attraction comes from our animal

22

brains, and it's all about play and pleasure. You need to enjoy the process and make sure the other person is enjoying it too. Laugh at yourself, don't take things too seriously, and let go of any hesitation around any ideas that seem kind of dated or sexist—love and relationships are messy, and, well, what works isn't always what our polite, rational mind likes to think is best.

Four Sequential Steps to Attraction

To delve more deeply into the instinctual markers of attraction, researcher Eric Waisman put forth a proposal of four specific components of attraction that shed some light on the sociobiological theory of attraction.

They are not hard rules, but rather general features people tend to look for in a partner, which happen to highly relate to biological drives. In the past, they represented a mate that was going to help you bear your children and protect them effectively. Articulating our subconscious desires is helpful in understanding why we are drawn to some people and even how we can improve our own attractiveness to the opposite (or same) sex. So, there is nothing we can do about our innate biological preferences, but we can gain insight into them and work with them.

Waisman's four types of attraction are:
1. Health
2. Status
3. Emotion
4. Logic

Interestingly, the order of those is also the chronological flow that must be followed for attraction to occur. This means each step is necessary for the next level of attraction to occur and to ultimately lead you into a relationship. When you've hit the fourth attraction factor, logic, it means you are compatible in all the preceding ways, and after the honeymoon dust settles, you will still be able to stand being around each other.

In a nutshell, here's how Waisman's attraction flow works:

You must first be physically healthy for anyone to take notice →
Next, you must be capable of providing what is biologically expected of your gender →
Next, you must be emotionally attractive and have romantic chemistry to feel lasting attachment →

NAV
MAGIC

Finally, a relationship can form if you share similar values, goals, and worldviews.

Once again, you don't have to look far to see the accuracy of these attraction types. They mirror the actual dating process almost exactly. If you spot someone at a bar or club, well, you wouldn't spot them if you didn't think they were physically attractive. Once you began talking to them, you'd feel more attracted to them if they had more power and status versus a career as a burger flipper.

After you'd gone out with them a couple of times, their dimples and physical attractiveness wouldn't be enough to sustain a relationship; you'd need to feel emotional bonding to them. But even all those prerequisites wouldn't be enough unless you had similar values and conceptions of how you wanted to live; if someone wanted to move to Alaska to hunt whales and your favorite movie was *Free Willy*, it might not work out.

Let's take a deeper dive into each part of the process. Step one is *health*.

When you meet someone, you first notice their physical appearance and attractiveness. At the very least, you notice if you find them physically unattractive or repulsive. More important, you notice if you are, or could be, sexually attracted to them. If you can't see them in that light, at least potentially, then the opportunity for attraction stops right there. The next levels don't even come into play because there would seemingly be no end goal.

It's why we groom ourselves, dress nicely, and go to the gym. We want to appear sexually viable, and we understand that shallow first impressions do indeed matter.

Of course, this is the origin of the so-called *friend zone*. Someone may check the boxes on the other types of attraction, but they aren't a sexually viable person, so there's really no amount of emotional support that can overcome that and they are generally doomed to friend status in perpetuity.

We are drawn to people we find physically attractive—not a radical idea. If you'd like to have sex with them or can imagine having sex with them, you've passed the first level of attraction.

It sounds shallow, and it might be, but it's how real-world attraction functions. It's only in romantic comedies that the hero ends up with the dumpy-looking best friend who has their best interests at heart! You can either play the game to win or decide to opt out and continually lose.

Most things we do to attract others target this attraction point because it's what people's first impression. Therefore, hitting the gym, making over your wardrobe, getting regular haircuts, trimming your nails, shaving occasionally, applying make-up, wearing high-heeled shoes—all help, no matter how much you want to believe otherwise.

If you don't quite like the idea of physical attractiveness playing such a big role (after all, not *everyone* is attractive, right? Certainly average and below average people have been hooking up happily since the dawn of time), then consider that *health* encompasses a little more than just appearances. If you are unremarkable in appearance but nevertheless seem fit, alive, and full of joy and vitality, that is attractive. A sulky underwear model with a bad attitude is only going to be attractive for point three of a second, while someone who is enthusiastic, bright, lively, and full of energy will likely be more appealing even if they're solidly average in appearance.

This is a clear, easy-to-read signpost for what we can work on. First impressions are made in a split second, so focusing your efforts on everything visible during that initial impression should be your first priority in becoming more attractive. If you understood that it was a true gatekeeper for you, how would you improve or change your appearance?

How viable of a mate would you appear to be if someone were basing their attraction to you on only this factor?

Step two: Is their status great enough for you?

This is commonly known as the resume phase—how do they look on paper? Being brutally frank, this is the phase that causes us to ask, "Are they beneath me? Will they be worth my time? Do they check the boxes that I am looking for?" Being less brutal: "Is this person like me? Do we fit in the same world? Are we in one another's league?"

After you're physically attracted to someone, the next step is to think about how eligible that person is and whether they will be able to provide for you in the way that you expect their gender to. No one wants their partner to be dead weight or a leech, and most people would like their partner to have the means to do the kinds of things they want to do. This isn't just about money, but money *is* certainly a large part of the equation. Status hearkens back to the sociobiological theory of women wanting support and safety and men seeking overall fertility.

The stereotypical gold digger would skip right to this attraction point, as would the stereotypical man looking for a trophy wife. The first two attraction points are the more superficial filters, and many a relationship has sustained itself on these for short periods of time. However, they may or may not be the most fulfilling or deep relationships.

Even though it's clearly important because none of us want to live in a shoebox, we lie to ourselves and refuse to give importance to this because we believe it instantly brands us as shallow and materialistic. But does it?

Evolutionarily speaking, no. Status began with wanting the leader of the pack, village, or tribe to ensure you would be protected and safe. You don't even have to come up with an analogy for that description to fit into the modern day.

Traditional gender roles play strong here. A man with status has power, money, and prestige. A woman with status has beauty, fertility, and nurturing instincts. It's a large part of the emotional bond that we like to deny, but evidence is available any time you venture into public. If there is a mismatch in physical attractiveness, often it's easy to see exactly why someone is with someone else.

The attraction of status is an evolutionary safeguard to survival.

The third factor essentially asks the following question: wait, do I actually *like* this person?

Do you have interpersonal chemistry, emotional attraction, and feelings of being drawn to them? Do you miss them when they aren't present? Do you share their sense of humor or at least appreciate their humor?

This is where *romantic love* finally comes into play—well, actually, scratch that. This is just where *getting along* comes into play. It might be surprising to see the notion of romantic love being demoted so far, but it's hard to deny that other factors take precedent, at least chronologically, before you can actually consider romantic love.

Look at the previous factors of health and status as the windows and windshield of a car. You can't drive the car without those, so you need to fulfill the basic needs first before you can hit the highway, so to speak. It's something we'd all like to imagine is our top priority when we're looking at a mate, but that's a lie that evolution likes to obscure with other types of attraction.

Romeo and Juliet certainly had emotional attraction, but look what happened to them. You can probably think of other examples where a couple seemed destined for each other but other factors tore them apart.

This naturally begs the question, if we're not marrying for love, what are we marrying for? It's time to expand the notion of love because it comprises many things that romantic comedy movies like to ignore.

Many of us allow feelings of romantic love and infatuation to take charge, but contrary to love songs, love is *not* all you need. There still remains the question of how truly compatible you are—not in personality, but in terms of worldview and values.

That's what the fourth stage is about: logic. You like (and maybe even love) each other, you get along well, you're physically attracted to each other, and you have a healthy financial prognosis.

But those are all still short-term concerns. What about thinking long term? Surely those aren't enough to sustain a marriage, are they?

It makes you ask questions such as:

- Can this relationship go the distance?
- Do we have the same life goals?
- Do we both want children?
- Do we share similar values?
- Will we be happy in five years?
- And perhaps most important, can I live with the other person's flaws or are they deal-breakers?

The logic phase questions whether it makes sense from a *rational perspective* to have a relationship with the other person.

The most common example of a relationship fizzling out because of logic is a vacation fling. Perhaps you've connected with another person, and everything seems incredibly in sync . . . but you've only spent forty-eight hours together and you live on opposite sides of the world. That's where logic steps in and sorts things out.

As you can see, the first two factors are more superficial and short-sighted, while the latter two factors are more introspective and indicative of a relationship's actual success.

Now visualize how many couples you know who have created relationships that depend solely on the first two (or three) attraction factors and have completely ignored the latter factors. It's no surprise that some couples fight like cats and dogs and are doomed to failure—they didn't align the types of attraction that matter long term.

Visualize a couple where the male wants children but the female does not. What does that mean for the long-term potential of that relationship, no matter how physically attracted they are to each other?

Logical attraction focuses primarily on our morals, values, and what is important to us in the world.

For example, do you want to get married? Do you want to have children after you get married? Do you have the same goals as far as career advancement and financial security are concerned? Do you want to live in Chicago forever or move around Asia for years at a time? Do you share the same religion?

Logic deals with deal-breakers.

We look at the people we can potentially date and sort them into yes and no piles based on their values. It's as simple as imagining whether a risk-averse corporate lawyer could ever truly be happy with a country-hopping nomadic soap salesman. Could they be attracted to each other?

This logical analysis is very linear. You look at core similarities and you project from there. The more you can imagine the possibility of a relationship, the more attractive the other person becomes.

The four attractions clearly spell out the steps you need to take to become attractive, and they prompt you to anticipate major issues that can become problems so that you can save your valuable time. Chances are, if you are skipping a step, you aren't an exception to the rule. You just haven't seen where the dust will settle.

Which among these four steps do you lack, and which are strengths you can capitalize on? Where in the process do you continually get stuck? These are the questions you can start to answer for yourself with your newfound knowledge.

Do Men and Women Want Different Things?

In reading the previous section, you might have wondered if the four sequential steps were always the same for all people at all times in their lives. Several studies show that there are indeed differences in the way that men and women appraise attractiveness in a mate, but even more than that, there are differences across age groups, meaning that even a single individual may change in their approach and their preferences over time.

A 2021 study by Stephen Whyte in the journal *PLOS One* found that men and women tend to choose mates according to three core areas: appearances, their personal characteristics and qualities (i.e., their personality), and resources (which includes income, education, and intelligence). Though the distribution patterns are similar, there are differences between men and women and between age groups. However, what remains the same is that men and women appear to rank and prioritize these areas in the same way.

Women are found to highly rate age, education, trust, emotional connection, intelligence, and income—around fourteen points more on a one-hundred-point scale than do men. Men, on the other hand, have a relatively higher preference for physical attractiveness and build compared to women.

SO IT IS INTER- ESTING THAT YOU CAN ATTRACT A 22 YO!

An interesting finding is that this difference between the sexes slowly diminishes with age; in other words, as people mature and get older, physical attractiveness becomes less and less important. On the other hand, the other two areas—personality and resources—become more important with age. This makes sense if we consider the four-step sequence above: physical attraction gets things started, whilst emotional connection keeps things going.

Basically, there are distinct differences between men and women, and this shifts across changing life stages. Evolutionary scientists talk about differing "parental investment" and how it impacts our mating behavior. In essence, because men and women have different biological roles in human reproduction, their behavior reflects their biological investment. But of course, this biological aspect itself changes over the course of our life.

What does this mean for people wanting to become masters at creating and sustaining attraction? Well, it means that you need to consider what "attraction" means for the people involved:

Are you male or female?
What stage of life are you in?
Are the people you want to attract male or female?
What stage of life are they in?

Seems obvious, but the answers to these questions will greatly affect the way you think about attraction and the strategy that will work best. For example, let's say you're a twenty-five-year-old single male with sex on the brain. You're in demographic who rates attractiveness and physical build in a mate the most highly. But who are *you* attracted to? Women the same age as you give lower rankings to attractiveness, and higher ones to personality and resources—in fact, the younger the women, the more she will prize traits like trust and emotional connection.

If you hope to get anywhere, your strategy needs to make sense. Yes, women in your desired age bracket value attractiveness to some extent, but they actually value emotional factors more. If you wanted a no-strings casual situation with a woman who didn't value emotional connection as much, you'd be better off going for a woman in her sixties!

This example simply shows that when it comes to the science of attractiveness, many variables are at play. What works best for you is going to be a balance between what you want and what you can offer. Some men are desperately unlucky in dating because they fail to consider "the market." Think of a creepy and unattractive-fifty-year-old divorced man who wonders why he can't catch a beautiful twenty-year-old heiress who is happy to spoil him financially. In this case, he's thought of what *he* wants but not how he appears to people he's attracted to and what *they* want, given their sex and age bracket.

Or imagine a woman who spends a lot of time primping and preening and going to the gym so she garners plenty of attention from young guys who highly rate physical attractiveness. She may catch one of these guys, only to realize that what she actually wanted was someone who she could rely on, talk to, and build a life with. Her strategy focused too much on how to be attractive while ignoring what she herself was attracted to, given her sex and age bracket.

What's your strategy?
You need to find the overlap between you and the person you hope to attract. You won't get anywhere trying to appeal to people in ways they don't actually care about. If you are a male, you need to understand that women rank attractiveness as *less* important overall than you do. They care about it, but they care about things too, so your strategy will fail if you don't recognize this and plan accordingly.

Do men and women want different things? Yes and no. We all want a partner who is attractive and smart and kind. But men and women prioritize these slightly differently. When you're dating, what you want is only half the picture—realize that what your mate finds attractive in you might be completely different!

Takeaways:

- The classic sociobiological theory of attraction states that we are nothing but animals when it comes to attraction. Worse yet, most of what we are attracted to is subconscious and not fully understood.

- Waisman's four steps are an elaboration on the classic sociobiological theory of attraction. They inform us as to exactly what we are looking for in a way that fuses sociobiological theory with modern dating.
- The four attractions are physical, status, emotion, and logic. It is a sequence you must pass through for a deep and fulfilling relationship, although we know many that only satisfied two or three factors in their own relationships.
- The best way to use these four factors is to understand what phase you are in when you are evaluating someone and to understand where you may fall short.
- Human beings tend to want the same things in their mates—attractiveness, resources, and emotional connection—but people will rank the relative importance of these differently depending on their sex and their life stage. A good dating strategy takes this into account and finds a workable overlap.

Chapter 2. Don't Say a Word

As you may or may not be aware, studies peg the importance of nonverbal body language this way: between fifty-five percent and ninety-three percent of the entire message we communicate to others is nonverbal and unrelated to the words coming out of your mouth. The amounts may differ from study to study and context to context, but the overall message is the same. It's not what you say; it's *how* you say it and how you look.

Naturally, this is going to transfer seamlessly to flirting and attraction, perhaps even more so because flirting involves a heavy number of cues and operates within gray areas. If this is important in everyday situations like school and work, imagine how important it is in engineering attraction and love, which reach down into our deepest and most primal relational urges.

The overall lesson of this chapter is to arm you with knowledge about what types of nonverbal body language are most attractive to the opposite sex, what to look for in evaluating the interest level of other people, and how to use this knowledge to make yourself attractive before you even open your mouth.

Various studies by Helen Fisher, Allen Pease, and Barbara Pease were able to articulate two main traits of body language that are both indicative of interest and attraction to others on an instinctive level and from an evolutionary standpoint.

Body Language

Surprisingly, the studies showed that the first aspect of attractive and effective body language is *availability*.

LEARN
THIS OBH

This means that you appear to be open, welcoming, friendly, and willing to engage. Smiles, uncrossed legs, eye contact, and a torso that is pointed fully toward the other person indicate availability. Think about it; how does someone who uses all of those body language gestures simultaneously appear to you? You would probably be less nervous to speak with them than someone with crossed arms and a mean look on their face. You'd feel that you would be welcomed instead of pushed away. You might feel like they are friendly and that you have a chance, which is always the first step to engaging.

Availability means there is, in theory, a decreased chance of rejection, and that is attractive because it feels as if it is within our grasp. If you have a chance, you're automatically more interested because it's more likely to be a better use of your time. Here, love and attraction shows itself as opportunistic.

How this comes across in body language is relatively simple—just be aware of closed and unavailable body language to start with. Start by eliminating the negative, and think about how open, vulnerable, and welcoming you make your body when you are approaching a puppy. It's a useful mental image for how to appear more available and overall attractive.

The second aspect of attractive and effective body language is how *fertile* you appear. *Fertile* is a term that refers to how powerful and effective a mate someone would be—as you can imagine, there are very different standards for men and women.

This goes back to understanding what we look for in each gender and the sociobiological theory of attraction from the previous chapter. Think back to traditional gender roles and the adjectives we use to describe each of them. What makes a man sexually attractive versus what makes a woman sexually attractive on a purely biological level? Now, how can you reflect those through your body language?

The body language of a biologically attractive man is dominant and powerful.

Attractive males embody the triangle-shaped body—broad shoulders that taper down to a thinner waist. They take up space with their shoulders and arms and try to emphasize their muscle mass with their posture. The bigger they can appear, the better (think of a peacock spreading its tail feathers). The more they can separate and distinguish themselves from other males, the better. The more dominant and deep the eye contact, the better.

Male fertility is about the ability to be a dominant mate who can protect his own, something that masculine body language signifies.

Males may also preen like peacocks, groom themselves, and make bodily movements to attract the attention of nearby females. It's all a show to draw attention to their alpha male traits. They compete for attention and mates, and everything is geared toward winning that competition.

Unsure what this looks like? Just imagine how differently a roomful of men would suddenly look if a supermodel walked in. Everyone's spines would straighten, stomachs would be sucked in, chests puffed out, and voices would deepen and get louder. They might each attempt to become the center of attention to show social influence and power. All this behavior might not even be conscious, but instinctually we understand that each gender is biologically programmed to project *fertile* body language.

If any men need guidance on how their body language should ideally be for flirtation and attraction, just think of the cartoon character

Johnny Bravo, but not so over the top. Everyone has their preferences, but the body language Johnny Bravo exhibits, with his huge upper body and expansive motions, is undeniably masculine and generally more preferred than a male that exhibits none of those things.

The ideal body language for a sexually attractive woman, on the other hand, is stunningly different.

In contrast to the triangle-shaped male, the female ideal is the hourglass figure. A woman is seen as more attractive if she appears graceful, soft, and curvy and slender at the same time. Femininity is all soft curves and supple flesh because female fertility is about the ability to give birth to multiple children and remain healthy.

Women want to accentuate the curves of an hourglass-shaped body. Put a woman in a pair of heels and have her walk past a row of attractive men. Notice how her gait changes, how it emphasizes her hips and bust and she suddenly acts like she is walking down a fashion runway.

Other indicators of fertility for females are the lips and hair—health is reflected in how healthy these physical traits are. This means the body language for an attractive female is to emphasize those physical traits and draw attention to them—hence lip-biting and hair-flipping.

If any woman needs guidance about how their body language should ideally be for flirtation and attraction, just think about Jessica Rabbit from the movie *Who Framed Roger Rabbit?* and how she saunters across a room. There's a reason so many men see her as the one cartoon they would sleep with without question.

This approach isn't about looking for specific signs—it's about thinking along the lines of availability and fertility. If you're still having trouble imagining how this plays out for the different genders, just imagine how ten women would pose for a picture versus how ten men would. They instinctively pop their hips and shoulders and attempt to create the illusion of curves and fertility to create a favorable hip-to-waist-to-breast ratio. You'll have a real-life illustration of how it plays out, and you'll be able to see exactly why the poses end up so differently. You can also consider how ancient Greek statues portray the different genders in a stark contrast of hard angles versus soft curves.

The vast majority of the messages we send to other people and to the world are nonverbal. Knowing the biological and evolutionary basis for what's attractive will help you see these signs and fulfill them yourself.

It's easy to overlook these aspects as "common sense" or as something you are already doing, but in reality, are you?

That's why it's so important to bring light to what have been proven to be objectively (as much as there can be in the field of attraction) attractive body language. Make sure you are ticking off the biologically proven triggers first, because it is unlikely you are acting in such an arousing way as to override people's evolutionary sensibilities.

Some people who struggle with attracting others are not objectively unattractive people. They may worry that the reason their love life is flatlining is because they need to look better somehow—they think if they were thinner/more buff/more tanned, then everything would work out for them, but rest assured: the attraction triggers discussed above are more negotiable than that.

If you are not naturally blessed with a tiny

waist or biceps that look like barrels, don't worry. Remember that flirting and attraction is about communication—we are sending conscious or unconscious messages to signal our health, our social and sexual availability, and our intentions. And a lot of this can be achieved with dress, posture, gesture, and body language. Marilyn Monroe, the quintessential sex bomb, was said to have blended into the crowd and been unrecognizable when she chose to be—she simply dressed down, dialed back her body language, and signaled her unavailability. Now, if Marilyn Monroe can make herself look plain and invisible, it stands to reason that people of average appearance can do a lot to make themselves more attractive and noticeable!

Eye Contact

Of course, eye contact is the other main component of how we perceive attraction and even rate it. As a society, we view eye contact as imperative to attracting a mate.

Surely, you've heard many times before that eye contact is *important. Eyes are the window to the soul, you can tell someone's goodness just by looking them in the eye, he wouldn't look at me in the eye and lie,* and so on. If you look up advice on dating, job interviews, sales, or just making friends, sustained eye contact will no doubt make the list as a key to what you want. We believe eyes convey emotion and empathy and that we can literally feel it from others when we lock eyes. BEND-YOU-OVER & FUCK-YOU SENSELESS EYES.

As a society, we place a lot of value on the implications of eye contact and what it means for trust in particular. If you meet someone who refuses to meet your eye contact, or conversely meets it for too long, you feel discomfort and leave with a negative impression of that person. People who don't make eye contact are perceived as being untrustworthy or deceitful. This ages-old assumption has been disproven repeatedly, most recently in 2012 in "The Eyes Don't Have It: Lie Detection and Neuro-Linguistic Programming" by Wiseman and Watt, which found no correlation between eye contact and deceit but instead a considerable correlation between hand gestures and deceit.

So while the lack of eye contact doesn't *actually* say anything about others, it may as well be true if people make those assumptions about you.

On the other hand, there is a truly significant number of positive assumptions that we make about people who make eye contact and that can surely improve people's perception of you. Generally, people who make eye contact are seen as more dominant and powerful; warmer and more personable; more attractive and likable; more qualified, skilled, competent, and valuable; more trustworthy, honest, and sincere; and more confident and emotionally stable. In other words, just about all the things that are associated with social success.

Why do we care so much about eye contact or the lack thereof? Is it just because we have been told from childhood to look at people in the eye and give them a firm handshake? Of course, it turns out that what may have started as old-fashioned advice from an older generation truly has many scientific confirmations.

In 1978 in "Effects of Eye Contact and Social Status on the Perception of a Job Applicant in an Employment Interviewing Situation," Tessler and Sushelsky found that we tend to make positive or negative assumptions based on how much someone meets our eye gaze—the more, the better.

In 2001 in "Accurate Intelligence Assessments in Social Interactions: Mediators and Gender Effects," Murphy and Hall found that we generally consider those who return eye contact to be more intelligent, conscientious, and sincere.

SINGERE AS WELL AS BYOL FYS

In 2016 in "Direct Speaker Gaze Promotes Trust in Truth-Ambiguous Statements," Kreysa and Kressler found that more eye contact promotes feelings of trust and genuineness.

Oddly enough, you probably knew the outcomes of these studies already. Whether they represent the truth or are just assumptions, we have to make sure that we don't fall on the wrong side of those studies.

EYES

As we are increasingly more caught up in a battle for our attention between our phones and our real-life conversation partners, the ability to make eye contact has become an especially powerful tool. When you can utilize eye contact smartly to show somebody that they have your undivided attention, you can effectively win them over and enhance their perception of you.

There was never a need to convince you about the role of eye contact in trust, but

52

there is one rather large caveat with eye contact—how should we use it? We can't simply stare into someone's eyes and try to read their souls. That is extremely uncomfortable and unsettling. In fact, eye contact has been shown to consume a significant amount of our brainpower and focus when we utilize it.

A 2016 Japanese study by Kajimura and Nomura titled "When We Cannot Speak: Eye Contact Disrupts Resources Available to Cognitive Control Processes During Verb Generation" found that eye contact consumes a significant portion of our general cognitive resources, and it is difficult to perform other actions, even talking, when making focused eye contact. If this is true for us, it is true for the person you are speaking to. Sustained eye contact is uncomfortable and causes a special kind of internal tension. This is probably why we feel the need to break eye contact when we want to remember something or explain something more complex. Give people a break.

In fact, in 2006, in a paper titled "Helping Children Think: Gaze Aversion and Teaching" by Phelps and Doherty-Sneddon, researchers found that kids told to look away while thinking and solving problems showed a 20%

increase in performance.

So how can we improve our eye contact to create feelings of trust? It has to start from the scientific evidence that people feel uncomfortable with a lot of sustained eye contact, but they also feel that you are a shady character if you don't provide enough. Where is the thin line where you are making your best impression and being most likable?

In 2016, Binetti and Hanson investigated the question of the average preferred length of eye contact. In "Pupil Dilation as an Index of Preferred Mutual Gaze Duration," they found that the average preference was only three seconds (before breaking contact and reengaging later). Most people preferred something between two to five seconds, and no one preferred anything under one second or over nine seconds. The thin line of eye contact appears to be that as long as you hold it for three seconds at a time, more often than not, then you will be seen as trustworthy. More eye contact is not better. Not even close to it.

In 1975 in "Eye-Contact, Distance, and Affiliation," Argyle and Dean observed that people tend to maintain eye contact roughly 40–60% of the time when conversing, and we should seek to maintain eye contact for 80% of the time. This leads us to my personal guidelines: make eye contact 50% when talking and 75% when listening.

INTERESTING, FOCUS ON EYES WHEN LISTENING

When you speak, you want others to be comfortable having their attention on you, but you also want to make sure that you don't appear to be hiding something or feeling uncomfortable yourself. And as you listen, you want whoever is speaking to see that you are engaged, but you don't want to look at them so much that they might feel creeped out. As long as you are in the general ballpark of 50% and 75% for speaking and listening, respectively, you'll be making the most out of the surprisingly powerful tool of eye contact.

The next level of creating attraction without saying a word is through touching, of course.

Strategic Touching

Is it a surprise that touch has a huge scientific basis for attraction? It's what causes our knees to wobble and butterflies to flutter around in our stomachs.

The lightest and subtlest touch, done correctly, can be the difference between seeing someone as a sexual object versus forever seeing them as only a friend. It can be a brush on the shoulder, a hand on the knee, and even a lingering handshake.

In the best (or worst) scenario, a touch can even make you light-headed and faint— maybe that's the origin of the phrase *starry-eyed love*?

So many people live in their heads. We rush around our daily lives, talking, working, living in abstract and hypothetical spaces, thinking, thinking, thinking . . . but we can be broken out of that spell when someone lightly touches us and reminds us that, at the end of the day, we are human beings who have *bodies.* TOUCH=HUMAN BEINGS

With how important touching is to courtship and attraction, it makes sense that there is an optimal way to touch others to enhance the attraction they feel for you. In fact, there are optimal ways, combinations, and types of touching that you should use to seduce others, male or female.

Your first step is to take a deep breath and break the touch barrier in general. Here's why: normally, acquaintances only touch in a particular, careful, unambiguous, mutually understood way. They shake hands or hug when they greet, or they might give a slap on the shoulder in acknowledgment of a joke or a job well done. These are all common and accepted ways of touching among people who know each other well and are friends or colleagues. There's only a certain threshold the touching will reach in a platonic manner.

Touching someone beyond that threshold instantly raises an eyebrow internally and instantly puts you into a different light. Touch alone can plant the seed of courtship. Attraction only works if you are seen as a sexual being, and sexual beings touch. Touching beyond that threshold sends an unambiguous message that there is attraction and interest. It's as close as you can get to saying that you are interested without using actual words. You wouldn't have to tell someone, "I like you and want to date you," if you always gave them extended hugs and put your hand on their knee during a movie. Think of it as taking that first step on the road that leads to full-on, reciprocal affection.

So when someone senses that, it's natural that they will begin to consider the toucher in that light as well. Touching also implies boldness, sexuality, and not being passive or shy—all of which are typically attractive in the opposite sex. Someone who is comfortable in their own skin can inspire others to relax into theirs, as well.

A big roadblock many people have with dating is falling into the friend zone—and the absence of touching is the very thing that leads them there. All other signs of interest or attraction are much more ambiguous and leave room for interpretation—touching sends just one message: I find you sexually attractive.

Now how can we touch strategically and effectively?

In a 2007 study by Nicolas Gueguen ("Courtship Compliance: The Effect of Touch on Women's Behavior"), scientists identified three distinct categories of touch and their different uses and consequences. They also found the exact combination to use to flirt and get your message across more effectively.

The three types of touching are:

1. Friendly touching
2. Plausible deniability touching
3. Nuclear touching

Let's discuss each of these in more detail.

58

The first category, *friendly touching*, is the type of touch I spoke about earlier, the kind you'd engage in with coworkers and friends. Actually, it's the type of touch you might even share with a stranger and give no second thought to because it's so casual and sometimes unavoidable.

Examples of friendly touching are handshakes, taps on the shoulder, a hand on the upper arm, high fives, and even bumping into someone else.

Friendly touching is intentional yet harmless. It doesn't advance attraction and in fact might be used to set a platonic tone. There is no subtext, and this kind of touching is exactly what it appears to be. It is not the kind of touching that sends a deeper message.

If you stick to this category of touch, it won't register at all that any flirting is occurring because it is so incidental and accepted. You could even do this with a stranger or someone you just met—although it's normally reserved for people you know (but not people you have a sexual or romantic interest in). There are no second thoughts given when you use friendly touch, and thus no attraction is created.

Obviously, this is the type of touch that is least related to attraction and flirting, but many people still attempt to send messages through it because they don't feel bold enough for other types of touch.

For example, thinking, "I touched his back for a split second longer as I was trying to get by him, so he definitely has to know what I'm thinking," is fairly common thinking—even though it was objectively the kind of touch you might use on a coworker to move past them in the hallway of your office.

Part of the problem with touching is it's mostly relative, which means that people have different standards for what constitutes "a lot" and "only a little" touching. This is why there are so many mixed and failed messages, even though these three distinct categories of touching exist. Learning to distinguish between the three types of touch will help you understand the exact type of message you are sending to others.

The second category of touch is called *plausible deniability touching*.

First things first—plausible deniability is when you create a situation where you could have a plausible claim that the touch was either unintentional or that it had no particular motive. So, yes, you've touched someone, but there is doubt about why you did so or whether you had any specific intention. The touch is over the threshold of a simple friendly touch, but you aren't sure if it was by accident or intentional—and the key is to get someone thinking about what you meant. Once you have people wondering, you're *in*.

People won't know what to make of you because your touching appears to be above the level of friendly touching—it definitely borders on flirtatious and deliberate, but the touching is contextual and incidental to some degree, so people are left wondering what you actually intended.

For example, buckling someone else's seat belt for them. This can be done in a relatively clinical manner, though your hands will definitely enter private zones on the other person's body. The plausible deniability here is just that you are in a hurry or you wanted to help someone buckle their seat belt. It raises eyebrows but is also acceptable in the context. Another example is when you fix someone's hair or find any flimsy excuse to be in a person's face or personal space.

Maybe you're there to make a move, or maybe you're there for a perfectly legitimate reason and you shouldn't be presumptuous!

You are in a gray area when you touch people this way, and that's effective because you can essentially touch a lot but not directly show your hand, so to speak. This is extremely effective for flirting and playing the game because you are sending an effective mixed message. On one hand, you are touching a lot and nearly violating their normal boundaries, but on the other hand, perhaps you just want to help them buckle their seat belt.

The important part is that they'll be thinking about you and your touch—you'll be on their mind. The first step to having sex with someone is to have them envision it, and that's exactly what this type of touch does. It makes a suggestion, but it also raises a question and makes your intentions mysterious enough to keep them wondering.

Flirting works best when there is a degree of uncertainty in the equation and you don't know exactly what the other person is thinking. It's like a game of cat and mouse, but each person thinks they are the cat. It's easy to see why plausible deniability touching can work wonders—the uncertainty is thrilling, just like a sports match would be far less interesting if you already knew the outcome.

Here are some additional opportunities for plausible deniability touching:

- Giving someone a brief shoulder massage
- Comparing the size of your hands (or other body part) with theirs by placing that body part next to theirs—as in placing your palms together
- Asking to examine something close to them, such as a piece of their clothing
- Holding someone's hip or waist to pull them in one direction
- Demonstrating a physical act (like a salsa dance move) on them
- Using your body to bump someone out of the way of something while you are walking together

Let your imagination run wild on this. Just remember that you need a plausible alternative explanation for being in someone's space, and your goal here is to be direct but also sow uncertainty.

The third category of touching as it pertains to flirting and attraction is dubbed *nuclear touching*.

This is where the rubber hits the road—there is no ambiguity here about your intentions and level of attraction. You meant to touch the person that way, and you meant something very deliberate by it.

Visualize a scenario where you know a kiss is imminent. What kind of slow, seductive touching would you use in the moments building up to that kiss? This is where you're making a statement and putting yourself out there for a potential rejection, which is something the other two types of touches explicitly avoid.

There are three main measures of nuclear-level touching. First, *where* are you touching? Nuclear touching occurs in zones that other types don't venture near. It's difficult to mistake your intent when you touch someone directly on their lips, grab their buttocks firmly, or pull someone between your legs. There can be no plausible deniability for any of those actions. Other areas that cause a nuclear reaction besides the obvious erogenous areas are the neck, face, and belly.

Second, is the touch by itself, or is it *combined* with other signs of attraction and flirting, like sustained eye contact and a lowered tone of voice? Touch by itself is one thing, but it is amplified when done simultaneously with other signs of deep attraction and flirting.

Third, how *deliberate* do you appear? For example, if you slid your hand onto someone's buttocks and they looked at you shocked, would you just smile and not move your hand, or would you immediately back off and apologize for being too forward? These two different responses from you demonstrate markedly different levels of intent and attraction.

Nuclear touching can be difficult to define, but you just know it when you see or feel it. You'll feel a rush of blood to your cheeks—and maybe elsewhere.

Now that you understand the three different categories of touching, is it possible to diagnose your flirting issues by the types of touch you've neglected or used ineffectively?

Perhaps you only use friendly touching and don't send the message you intend to. You'll think you are subtly sending a message, but in reality, you are just treating someone like a new friend. Or maybe you use nuclear touching too much and it scares people off or makes you seem predatory and overly aggressive.

The study went on to suggest that the most effective type of touching is actually a combination of plausible deniability and nuclear touching, with friendly touching not making much of an impact at all.

This shouldn't be surprising if we consider that flirting thrives in uncertainty and creates a push (they like me) and pull (they don't like me), and this combination creates the very same effect. The power is in the combination, because each type, used by itself, doesn't convey the message you intend.

For example, friendly touching by itself just makes you appear to be the friendly type at work or in social situations.

If you overuse plausible deniability and never let it slide into nuclear touching—so that there is no question of your intent— eventually the other person will lose interest. They will assume you are either clumsy or without couth; they won't assume you have an interest in them. You will have disguised yourself too well!

If you use nuclear touch too much, it can be too direct and aggressive and will not create mystery for the other person to wonder about. Or you'll just get slapped. If you make your intentions too direct and don't give them a chance to process things for themselves, their fight-or-flight mode will be activated. They might just panic and retreat.

If there is a single lesson to be taken from this chapter, it's that you have to make yourself a sexual object. This is the biggest failing of the so-called friend-zoned men and women— they hope to show their potential as a mate through everything but sex. But we are, at our root, just hairless primates that want sex—so make yourself sexually viable with touch, body language, and eye contact.

LIKE WITH THE EYES, SEXUALISE WITH TOUCH

Playing Hard to Get

You probably don't need much introduction to this classic dating strategy. This approach to getting people to be more interested in you is so familiar to people because, frankly, it's a common one, and it usually works. The idea is that you want to convey the impression that you are a very valuable mate indeed, and the more desirable you are, the more other people will want you.

How do you we know that someone is a

desirable mate? Well, they seem "hard to get." They're not easy, they're not overly available, and they're not automatically going to be around. A desirable person is seen as in high demand and as though they have their own busy lives elsewhere. When you play heard to get, you induce this feeling in another person that you are something precious and quite special, and that it will take a little effort to win you over. Creating an illusion of scarcity and value, you raise your esteem in other people's eyes. Sure, it's old school, but it's one aspect of the dating game that doesn't seem to be going anywhere.

Researchers explored this phenomenon from an economics model of dating, where they see the person playing hard to get as the "supply" and the person doing the getting as the "demand." It doesn't take a genius to see that by manipulating the perception of the supply, you can increase demand.

It's all about perceived availability. A team of researchers from the University of Rochester found that creating a sense of uncertainty into the chase actually does work to increase the perceived value of a mate and thus increase our desire. While it seems like a good idea to immediately reciprocate any interest shown in you, in some cases, "playing games" may be beneficial, at least in the early stages of dating where you're building that crucial attraction.

Simply being aloof and unavailable is unlikely to work long term, and continually blowing hot and cold can backfire, so it's important to understand that the goal is not simply to be mean but to increase your perceived value. Let's look at what the researchers found actually increased a person's perceived value as a mate.

Those who were perceived to be more *selective* in their own dating criteria came across as more high value. Think about it this way—which club will seem more valuable, the one that lets anyone in or the one that's a bit more choosy? If you appear to be choosy, it implies that you have options, which in turn implies that you are generally valuable.

Another interesting finding was that people generally felt someone was more worth their time if they were asked to invest more into their acquisition of that person's time. When people are made to try their best, be a little convincing, and "earn" something, they can't help but feel that it's more valuable to them than those things they attained easily. If you've invested effort into a relationship, you're more likely to view that relationship, and therefore that person, as more valuable. In other words, you're more likely to make great efforts to see someone again if you've made great efforts to see them in the first place. COMFORT INVESTMENT = 10 MIN

Generally, the researchers concluded that playing hard to get did in fact increase a person's mate value in other people's eyes. But not always! Used carelessly, this approach could send mixed signals and frustrate or bore the person you're trying to attract.

Remember that you don't want to be arrogant or mean. You simply want to appear in demand, selective, and as though you have other options. It's usually best to show interest early on, but just because you've flirted a little, it doesn't mean you must suddenly be one hundred percent available with no uncertainty as to your feelings at all.

Instead, play with the tension between revealing yourself and getting close, but also pulling back occasionally to pursue your own life, take a breather, and allow that tension to build up again. Remember that people, by definition, cannot want what they already have. So, when you create a little distance, it's not so you can feel superior or control the other person, but rather so that you can create a wonderful sense of tension that is then released when you do connect with them again. GREAT STUFF

- Don't always reply instantly to messages
- Avoid saying yes to invitations immediately—even if you are available, pretend you need to check your calendar first
- When you are with the other person, lavish your full attention on them, but have limits—for example, say you have plans later that afternoon. You want to give the impression that they are lucky to enjoy a moment in your full and busy life.

Allow your partner to sometimes wonder about you, rather than assuming you're "in the bag." Let anticipation build. Play with a little uncertainty. You'll notice that none of this requires you to be rude or haughty! Finally, playing hard to get is something that is best limited to the early days of a relationship, or for casual encounters only. In a longer term relationship where you are both assured of one another's interest and attention, there is a certain degree of

 NAVI

familiarity and certainty, but you can still maintain your own independence, and you can still ensure that there is a little mystery, tension, and distance to keep things interesting.

The Thrill of Uncertainty

Take a look at the following scenarios:

Scenario 1: You go on a first date with someone, have a great time, and then are doing the date "postmortem" afterward to assess how it went. You liked her, but you aren't exactly sure about how she felt about you.

Scenario 2: You go on a first date, have a great time, and learn later that your date also had an amazing time and is very keen to meet you again.

Which woman are you most attracted to? Though you might think that you'd prefer the woman who was obviously as into you as you were into her, research in the journal *Psychological Science* actually suggests that people are more attracted to those who seem undecided about them. In other words, uncertainty may increase feelings of attraction more than clearly knowing someone else's feelings.

The study asked women to rate their attraction to different men, but with researchers apparently manipulating the degree of attraction they themselves felt for the women. The results were interesting: women were very attracted to those men who they believed were attracted to them. But most surprising was that the women were even more attracted to those men whose feelings for them were uncertain. So, openly declaring your attraction for someone is a great strategy, yet it's not as good as remaining a little "mysterious"!

REMAIN MYSTERIOUS

The scientists called this the "pleasure" of uncertainty—although if you've ever experienced the agony of not quite knowing if your feelings are reciprocated, you might disagree with how pleasurable it is! What is clear is that is does in fact increase your attraction. It's as though the unresolved nature of the situation grabs our attention. Cognitively, the issue remains unresolved, so our thoughts return again and again to the other person, trying to figure them out. Contemplating whether he "loves me or loves me not" may in fact be more pleasurable and create more feelings of attraction than being

CREATE UNCERTAINTY

flattered outright or (obviously) rejected by your love interest.

All this is to say that uncertainty is a part of the dating game, and, if you do it right, an especially fun and exciting way to build tension and create attraction. The key is to remember that you are *building* attraction and piquing interest, not squashing it. You never want to give the impression of outright rejection, but rather keep things open ended. It's the game of trying to find out what the other person feels for you that builds attraction. The idea is to create uncertainty, which makes you pop up in the other person's head as often as possible, which in time kindles attraction. It may even be that once you do reveal your interest and end the uncertainty, there is a greater sense of accomplishment and resolution—remember, the things we perceive as scarcer or more effortful are things we perceive as more valuable.

What can we do with the results of such a study? Well, the first thing is not to openly display too much affection too early on. Interest and politeness—yes. But you want to retain some mystery, and leave a little room open for the chase. Never make yourself seem like a "sure thing." That way, the other person has you on their mind. Even better if you can build in a little flirting that plays with the very idea of not quite being sure yet where you stand with one another.

NEGGING: FOR THE SUPER-HOTTIES

A word on the common technique of "negging" or actively putting a woman down to build attraction—it doesn't work. The study found that when women perceived that men did not in fact find them attractive, they seldom felt attracted themselves. It's usually a bad idea to insult women—even playfully! Women love being complimented—remember that this absolutely increased the attractiveness of men in the eyes of the women in the study. But if you want to build attraction *even more*, don't start making declarations of attraction too soon in the game. You may choose to share a few compliments but make them ambiguous, so that she doesn't quite know what these compliments mean.

It's all about dynamic tension—you are concealing the extent of your feelings not to play games or manipulate, but rather to create a deliciousness and expectation—a bit like how concealing a Christmas present with wrapping paper makes us more excited to receive it than simply getting it immediately with no need to wait and wonder what's inside and whether we'll like it or not!

Why Breaking the Rules Can Be Attractive

Who is sexier, the person who boldly puts their feet on the table despite what anyone thinks, or the person who follows all the norms of social etiquette? The person who is happy to bend the rules when they like, or the person who is strict about adhering to them?

A paper published in the *Journal of Social Psychology and Personality Sciences* in 2011 shared findings after Van Kleef et. al. investigated whether people who violate norms are perceived by others as more powerful. They set up various groups to perform certain minor rule violations (like putting your feet on the table) and observed people's responses, finding that it tended to signal a certain degree of power to others.

The authors of the study noted that it probably wasn't the specific rule that was broken that was important, but rather the attitude that its breaking implied—we respond when we see a person behaving as though they have the freedom and power to behave as they will, no matter the constraints put on them or what other people's rules are.

It makes sense, but does it apply to dating and relationships?

Importantly, the study concluded only that minor rule-breaking behavior was associated with *power*. It is a separate step to assume that an increase in perceived power also increases *attraction*. I'm sure you can imagine a situation where you perceive that someone possesses power in some sense, but that doesn't mean you like or even respect them.

Dating coaches and behavioral psychologists alike have long known that competence and capability are attractive to members of both sexes (we'll look at universally attractive traits in a later chapter). In other words, we like people who know what they're doing and who are confident in their ability to do it. Whether they are physically strong, intelligent, skilled in some way, or possess an admirable talent, such people can convey a sense of confidence and self-assuredness that is attractive.

So, that person who puts their feet on the table may be signaling this very thing: a confidence in one's own will, and a willingness to go along with that rather than other people's rules and agendas. That's powerful, and it's sexy.

But you can guess the caveat coming up: nobody likes a jerk. We'll see later in the book that kindness, helpfulness, and genuine compassion are always attractive. But if you want to try being a rule breaking to be more attractive, bear a few things in mind:

- Don't break the big rules and completely violate the social contract. Telling a little white lie or speeding now and then can be endearingly human, but obviously outright criminal actions will only signal that you're bad news and should be avoided.
- Don't break rules just for the sake of breaking them—you won't look like a cool rebel, but rather like a bratty child trying to get a reaction. Instead, break rules according to what genuinely makes sense for your values. This sends a message that you have values, you trust your own judgment, and you won't succumb to convention, peer pressure, or habit quite so easily.
- Never break rules when it means violating someone's boundaries. Feel free to lie a little on your tax return,

walk on the grass instead of the path, or smoke in the hotel bathroom. But ignoring people's personal boundaries doesn't make you powerful—it makes you a bully! A bully who gets a kick out of pushing people's buttons is in fact unconfident and insecure.

- The best kinds of rules to break are those that you suspect everyone wants to break anyway. Choose those things that are a *little* bit naughty, but don't actually cause any harm. Choose those rules that don't actually make much sense and are just begging to be broken. You're not being aggressive or arrogant, but rather playful and irreverent.

- Finally, you can be more attractive simply by *not* being the boring conformist always fearful sticking to the rules no matter what. Don't be a wet blanket! You'll send the message that you value other people's will and intentions more than your own, or that you lack confidence in your own abilities or perceptions. Don't be that person who is always monitoring and chastising others—it's a total turn off.

Understanding this principle means you can apply it elsewhere, too. A great flirting technique is to playfully encourage others to break rules with you—you create a brief sense of intimacy and fun and now have a shared secret. You also let the other person know that you're not a stick in the mud and won't be judgmental of their foibles. You come across as confident, resilient, and good-humored—and they feel they can let their hair down with you, too.

Takeaways:

- Many animals don't have verbal languages. This means they must communicate their attraction, often forcefully, through their movements and actions. The human equivalent is how we communicate nonverbally with our body language, eye contact, and touching.
- There are different types of attractive body language for each gender. They do, however, depend on the factors of availability and fertility. Simply put, the more available you appear, the more attractive you will be, and the more fertile (this varies by gender) you appear, the more attractive you will be.
- When we think about trust, one of the first places our minds will go is to eye contact. Whatever the reality, if you aren't able to use eye contact, people will find you

untrustworthy. Thus, eye contact has been found to cause people to attribute positive traits to you and see you as more intelligent and more trustworthy. But how do we wield eye contact without creeping people out or appearing untrustworthy? The thin line appears to be around three seconds of eye contact at a time, with sufficient rest between gazes.

- There have been found to be three types of touching in the context of flirting and attraction: friendly, plausible deniability, and nuclear. The most ideal mix is plausible deniability touching mixed with nuclear touching because of the message it sends and how it balances itself out. Friendly touching doesn't really factor into it, even though that's what we are most accustomed to.

- Playing hard to get is a proven tactic for increasing attraction, because it can increase your perceived value. Be careful about being mean or arrogant, though— you want to build pleasurable anticipation and expectation.

- You may appear more attractive when people are unsure of your feelings for them, so don't be too transparent too early on. Give compliments, but let their meaning be ambiguous.

- Breaking rules can be attractive since it conveys confidence and power and communicates that you act from your own internal integrity, which is sexy! Never violate people's boundaries, however, and cause any actual harm.

Chapter 3. The "Chase"

Dating advice is one of the most prevalent topics in the world.

No matter where you go and no matter the culture you enter, there will always be magazines and books about how to have more success in dating. Why is that?

There are the obvious reasons: that sex, dating, marriage, and everything that follows is a huge part of what we want out of life. They are some of our primary motivators and consume much of our mental bandwidth every day. They represent many of our hopes, dreams, and aspirations and are the cause of many of our greatest triumphs and failures. Whether we realize it or not, we are always priming ourselves for attraction and the possibility of mating in some way or another.

But the other underrated reason dating advice is so prevalent is because it is the epitome of *shades of gray*. There are an almost infinite number of interpretations for every single action because everyone brings their own bias and anecdotal experience to every situation. There can be endless debate, and everyone seems to have an opinion about what to do in certain circumstances. After all, some people like dogs and some like cats. And how much more complicated dating is! There are countless interpretations, perspectives, and opinions, and each of them is likely to be "right" in some way. The fact is, few people are *subjectively wrong* in their opinions, which further stokes the flames of discussion and debate.

For example, strong eye contact is highly preferred and seen as confident in Western cultures but is threatening and directly confrontational in some Eastern cultures. But it spans beyond obvious cultural differences as well. I might think that my simple act of putting my hand on a woman's back is casual, but she might interpret it as incredibly forward and borderline "creepy" because she was raised in a household where her parents showed no physical affection for each other.

As human beings, we all crave connection, physical intimacy, and to share our lives with others. However, these basic and primal biological drives are pushed through complex cultural and sociological filters, and this is why advice on the "rules" varies so much. The underlying point is that you can never be certain that your message will be received as you intended—or received at all. This is especially true in the process of flirting and *chasing*, where you don't want to come on too strong, or be weakly and forgettable.

ABUNDANCE MENTALITY

The Chase

What is *the chase*? There are countless definitions of it.

1. Implanting the idea of your romantic interest in someone so they end up pursuing you
2. How to attract someone covertly and indirectly
3. Conveying romantic interest in a slick and sly way
4. A mind game between two interested parties designed to make the other act first and show their cards
5. How to utilize hot and cold, push and pull behavior to entrance someone

romantically

6. How to calibrate the right amount of romantic interest in someone to ignite their attraction to you

Hopefully, one or all of those definitions resonates with you—they all describe mostly the same situation or feeling that we try to create. The above come from different models for understanding attraction, but as we've said, though the models may differ a little, they all speak to an underlying understanding of an objective fact in the dating world: the connections we desire with others are seldom spontaneous or effortless, and usually if we want to interact with the people we desire, we need to *do something* to make that connection happen. What that "something" is varies widely.

Here's what it boils down to: you want to create attraction with others, but you can't show *too much* interest; otherwise, you appear too available and low value. But you can't show *too little* interest, because then people might not even notice your overtures. Basically, you want to strike the right balance of attention and availability for people to see you in the most attractive light. This is extra tricky because, as we've seen, there are unknowns and a lot of guesswork involved.

Even for the people who say that they hate the chase and playing games, they have to admit that they instinctively do things differently when they want someone's attention or affections. There are more passive and indirect ways to induce someone else to take action and come to us, but it all comes down, one way or another, to us chasing what we want.

SHOW HER THAT'S SHE GONE OFF YOUR RADAR!

Something odd happens in our minds when someone is too available, too interested, and too eager—and we don't want to be that person! The opposite happens in our minds when someone is unavailable, aloof, and ambiguously interested. We instantly begin to wonder what we're missing and what could be at stake if they suddenly lost interest. We feel like we need to chase them a bit to get back on their radar.

Just imagine how you felt when you knew that someone was *very* interested in you. You might actually be slightly repulsed and turned off. Now imagine that same person showed only occasional signs of interest in such a way that you were never truly sure how they felt about you. How do these situations color your perception of their value? The former makes you question their worth if they are so easy to attain and available. The latter makes you question yourself and your own feelings.

Why do we want what we can't have or aren't certain to attain? Why do we chase or subconsciously try to compel others to chase us? Uncertainty and novelty drive us, while predictability causes complacency and disinterest. The psychological underpinnings of this have been proven over and over in the past century, but first in 1952 by B.F. Skinner in "Intermittent Rewards in Operant Conditioning."

In his landmark study, he provided one group of lab mice with a reward every time they pressed a lever, while another group of mice obtained a reward only randomly after pressing a lever.

The first group received consistent reinforcement, while the second group received intermittent reinforcement, and Skinner discovered that intermittent reinforcement caused the mice to press the lever at a much greater rate than those who received consistent reinforcement.

This tells us that the mice who were rewarded consistently ended up taking it for granted because they knew it would be waiting for them whenever they wanted. They likely got bored because part of the reward for pressing the lever was the anticipation of the reward itself. Whatever the case, they stopped trying as much. The mice who were rewarded inconsistently didn't know when their next reward would come, so they kept pressing the lever to ease their uncertainty.

Coincidentally, this is also the exact psychology behind why gambling and slot machines in particular are so addictive—if you don't know when your reward is coming, you'll be motivated to keep searching for it. Once you finally receive a reward, you'll be immediately looking for your next one because you are so unsatisfied with how long it took.

Intermittent reinforcement is what we try to accomplish with the chase. We are trying to present ourselves as ambiguously available in order to get someone else to pursue us and become fixated on us. We want to give people just a taste so they are unsatisfied and continue to seek you out for more attention or contact. If you think about your behavior during your pursuit, you'll realize that this creed informed many of your actions.

Observe the chase in action:

- We delay texting back immediately.
- We pretend to be busier than we really are.
- We make our weekends sound more fun than they actually were.
- We avoid people sometimes even though we want to see them. AVOID SEEING PEOPLE
- We don't tell people we like them or care about them even though we do.

We generally attempt to manipulate how available and interested we seem because that's what creates the sense of intermittent reinforcement.

Let's see what constant, consistent reinforcement looks like.

You meet someone with whom you instantly hit it off. You grew up in the same small town just minutes away from each other, and they share your love of noir fiction and old black-and-white movies.

No games this time, you decide. You've wasted too much of your life strategizing, so you're going to be straightforward and skip the chase.

So you text them immediately after you get home, and then again in the morning when you wake up. You tell them your entire week is free. You reply to their texts within seconds and tell them about how much your family will like them. You ask whether they like Mexico or Greece for next summer's vacation.

Every time you contact them, they start to look at their phone in disgust because it's too much, too soon, and they've grown tired of the reward you are providing. We prefer a little mystery and intrigue; thus, the more in demand someone is, whether it's work, dating, or friend-related, the more attractive they become.

Of course, instead of spending all this time and effort cultivating an image of a busy person who is in high-demand and unavailable, your time is far better spent actually *being* that high-value person: The type who actually needs to wait hours to text back because they are so occupied. The type who truly only has three free nights in the next two weeks.

Instead of plotting your text timelines and how to reply, become the person that is too busy with their friends, family, hobbies, and passions. It's counterintuitive, but when you're engaged, you become absolutely engaging. Playing the game can feel icky to some, so that's the least positive interpretation of it.

You might not enjoy utilizing the chase, but if you're going to date, at least play to win—in other words, create a sense of intermittent rewards and mystery.

People say they don't like to play games. If, they say, you can't make someone like you by conventional means, then you didn't deserve them in the first place. Ask people who have been friend-zoned repeatedly how that's worked out for them. Knowing what people are psychologically attracted to is undeniably effective and can often help you cross the line between nothing and a relationship.

Unavailability

Closely related to intermittent reinforcement and the chase is the reality that humans want what we can't have or don't currently possess. It's not logical, it's not smart, but that's humans for you!

We know this to be true because we have sudden feelings of regret when our attractive friends get into relationships—even friends we might never have considered as romantic prospects before that moment. It's just human nature to wonder, *What could we be missing out on?*

This was proved in a study by Parker and Burkley. One group of women was presented with a photograph of a handsome man and told he was single, while another group of women was presented with the same photograph and told he was married. Fifty-nine percent of the women were interested in pursuing the single man, but ninety percent wanted to pursue the married man.

PLAY THE GAME

We want what is unavailable to us, especially if we see other indicators of its value and demand. In a vacuum, we may want only what we want, even if no one else wants it. But if someone or something is wanted by many people, then we want it even more. We want to discover for ourselves *why* they are so desirable and ensure we're not missing an integral piece of information.

When something is easily within our grasp, instead of basking in the triumph of getting it, we think *"Wait, is this even worth having if it's so easy? Could I do better?"* and we don't want it anymore. When that same thing is removed from our realm of possibility or even just made more difficult to attain, we aren't sure if we can attain it, so we feel compelled to keep trying. Marketers understand this principle keenly, and that's why you'll see adverts offering a limited time offer, or a deal that is exclusive and hard to find, invite only or otherwise in demand yet scarce.

This is the essence of playing hard to get. Just remember that you can't play *too* hard to get; otherwise, you'll appear uninterested and people will give up. People's perception of what is valuable will correlate to the pride and sense of achievement they get when they attain that valuable thing, but if the valuable thing is so far out of grasp it's impossible to ever achieve, the opposite is likely to happen: sour grapes and devaluing the unreachable goal. It's *hard* to get, not *impossible* to get.

Studies by Jonason and Li in 2013 identified the types of behaviors that people used when they consciously played hard to get. Do any of these sound familiar?

- Not expressing affection toward their target
- Talking with, flirting with, and even dating

94

other people
- Giving accidental physical contact
- Sarcastic but friendly teasing NOT RUDE OR MEAN
- Making others work to spend time with them
- Acting artificially busy
- Flirting and then disappearing; giving attention and then stopping
- Acting disinterested
- Taking a long time to reply to calls or texts

The researchers also asked if these tactics worked in attracting someone they were interested in. They did—every single one of them.

Subjects then rated which respondents (low, medium, high availability) were most attractive to them in given scenarios. High availability was only desirable for short-term relationships. Low availability was just discouraging or preoccupied. The medium availability potential partner was rated the most attractive because they represented someone that was in high demand but was still possible for them to attain. When a person like this gives you attention, it feels valuable.

The old dating advice "treat 'em mean to keep

'em keen" is just a crude way of expressing a very real tendency in in people. It's not that being unkind or playing games is necessary—rather that certain behaviors are legitimately associated with "high value" people and that we can improve our chances at love when we consciously work with these tendencies and put ourselves in the best possible light.

Shining a flashlight onto the games we subconsciously play may not always be pretty, but it is helpful for you to get who you want. Usually when we turn to games, we have a clear direction of where we want to go. In fact, most of the time, we want to avoid the situation you're about to read about.

"Let's Just Be Friends"

The first time I heard that phrase uttered, I was fourteen years old. I was crushing on a girl in my Spanish class, Miranda, and I had made an effort to be extra nice to her, help her with her homework, and generally treat her with more attention than I had probably treated any female in my life besides my mother. I began to classify us as close friends.

The whole process began in December, and I remember January turning into February.

This was significant because February is the *money* month—it's got Valentine's Day, which was going to be my greatest opportunity to knock her socks off with my grand romantic gestures and make her fall for me.

Remember, I was fourteen, so let's lower expectations here. I asked my mother to take me to a florist where I bought flowers. I also bought a box of discounted See's Candies because my mother would only allow me to spend twenty dollars on my grand gesture for Miranda.

When Spanish class rolled around on that fateful Valentine's Day, I tapped her on the shoulder and presented her with the flowers and chocolates that had been stuffed into my locker for most of the day.

Her reply? "Let's just be friends." It was a dagger to the heart that took me quite a while to recover from. Is this something you can get around? Is it a real truth that men and women can be truly platonic friends without any romantic complications? Does the chase work here?

The politically correct answer may be to proclaim you can indeed be platonic friends forever. Friendship and sexual attraction are two entirely different measures, and people can separate the two without too much trouble. People can compartmentalize emotions, and people can support and be emotionally intimate with others without romantic or sexual feelings being involved. Friendship is a bond that can transcend base desires.

Platonic opposite-sex friendships might even be important for our psychological health. Famed psychologist Carl Jung put forth the theory of animus and anima—animus refers to male energy present within females, and anima refers to female energy present with males. Part of the reason we gravitate toward opposite-sex friendships, beyond mating, is to connect with these parts of our personality that balance us.

If you don't agree that men and women can be platonic friends, then the underlying message is that emotion isn't easily separable. Friendship, affection, love, support, and intimacy are all heavily interrelated, so sometimes sex is just a stone's throw away from a close friendship. Friendship itself might arise because there is underlying sexual attraction—in other words, sometimes we become friends with members of the opposite sex as a long-term road to having sex with them.

In 2012, researchers surveyed a group of heterosexual males and females about their opposite-sex friendships, and the results suggest a combination of the two views is correct (Bleske-Rechek et al., 2012).

For the females, there was a harsh divide. They were able to view a friendship as purely platonic or a romance in waiting. Males, on the other hand, seemed unable to disassociate their opposite-sex friendships from the idea of sex or the possibility of sex with their female friends.

In the same vein, males were more likely than the females to perceive sexual interest from their opposite sex friends, while women perceived the opposite. Men saw signs of a potential sexual relationship embedded everywhere in a friendship, while women reported signs of a platonic relationship everywhere. The women interpreted sexual interest as friendliness, while the men interpreted friendliness as sexual interest. In a purported platonic friendship, this implies that, most of the time, males operate under ulterior sexual motives.

According to this study, the chase may not

save you here, at least if you are a male, it seems. If a woman has made up her mind, you may be stuck without a hope.

For males, being "just a friend" almost always has undertones of "a friend that I haven't had sex with yet." This doesn't mean there can't be a flourishing friendship or that the parties can't mutually benefit in huge ways, but it may stun women to learn that many of their male friends are only their friends because they have a pull of sexual attraction to them. It doesn't always mean they want more than friendship, but it does indicate their motives aren't always innocent.

Women don't hold this perspective and appear to be able to whole-heartedly have platonic feelings toward men. It would be easy to throw blame at the evolutionary imperative males have to view every female as a potential child bearer and maximize their opportunities, but I think the reason is much simpler these days. The social dynamics of any party will demonstrate it—males compete for females, while females don't compete as much for men. Simple logic dictates that men are actively surrounding themselves with women that they want to have sex with, while women are not.

Men and women certainly can be great friends, but the impulse that built these friendships can be very different. But if you meet a goal and each party is satisfied with their withdrawal from the relationship bank, does it matter how the goal was met?

Men have friendships based on sexual attraction, regardless of whether it is plausible or fulfilled. A man's friend circle is full of women he is sexually attracted to, but for various reasons he may or may not act on his desires. This shouldn't devalue the friendships; it's just the impetus for seeking them out in the first place. If a male doesn't find a female sexually attractive, it doesn't mean that an amazing friendship cannot blossom. But sexual attraction is a primary motivator for males.

Very rarely do men forego this so-called shallow approach. Women on the other hand appear to view men in a far more holistic manner, and attractiveness by itself is not a significant factor in choosing their opposite sex friends.

Of course, same-sex friendships avoid most of these problems and bring their own special benefits. Relationships between females are fraught with more combined oxytocin, which creates a network of support, intimacy, and empathy that is literally lacking from male bloodstreams (Taylor and Klein, 2000). Male relationships, on the other hand, are somewhat more primitive, much like their view of females as sexual opportunities. Aristotle put it this way:

> *Perfect friendship is the friendship of men who are good, and alike in virtue; for these wish well alike to each other equal good, and they are good themselves . . . But it is natural that such friendships should be infrequent; for such men are rare.*

> *Further, such friendship requires time and familiarity; as the proverb says, men cannot know each other till they have "eaten salt together"; nor can they admit each other to friendship or be friends till each has been found lovable and been trusted by each. Those who quickly show the marks of friendship to each other wish to be friends, but are not friends unless they both are lovable and know the fact; for a wish for friendship may arise quickly, but friendship does not.*

The movie *When Harry Met Sally* famously proposed that men and women can be platonic friends with no romantic intentions. It's a romantic comedy so it was inevitable that Billy Crystal and Meg Ryan end up together, but science backs it up completely.

The Deeper the Love, the Deeper the Hate

Most of us consider love and hate to be, well, opposites. We see them as extremes on the far ends of a continuum. A 2017 study done in the journal *Frontiers* by Jin, Xiang, and Lei examined the relationship between love and hate and had some interesting findings. The first finding was that similarity between partners was predictive of love in a couple (we'll say more about similarity in a later chapter). The second finding was that these stronger feelings of love were correlated with increased feelings of hate after a relationship ended or broke down.

What shall we make of these findings?

The authors of the study examined the idea of betrayal as a third variable and found that it was a sense of betrayal that usually brought about the feeling of hate in a relationship where there was once love. If someone you loved betrayed you, the feeling of hate that emerged would be in proportion to the degree of your prior love. This makes intuitive sense. If you open up and trust someone, become intimate with them, and then feel that intimacy and trust betrayed, you are likely far more hurt by the experience than if the person had merely been someone you were lukewarm about. It's kind of impossible to full-on *hate* someone who you never had any other strong feelings for before, right?

So, perhaps studies like these hint at a different interpretation, i.e., that love and hate are not really opposites at all. Instead, love and hate have a lot in common in the fact that they are both intense emotions liable to emerge in the context of, and as a consequence of, intimate personal relationships. Neither love nor hate are associated with acquaintances, though. The most you'll ever feel is mild irritation or being a little pleased, but this is not the realm of strong emotion.

Let's imagine what we can do with this insight and how to put it into context with the "chase." Have you ever noticed in many romance stories that the heroine often starts out actively loathing the main love interest?

Sometimes, a pair decidedly rub one another up the wrong way . . . before miraculously finding themselves rubbing one another the *right* way. Why?

That's because strong emotion—even if it's hate or annoyance—is closer to love than it is to indifference.

SPIKEY EMOTIONS

Now, this isn't to say that the way to someone's heart is to make them hate you first, but rather that it's better to think in terms of general *emotional arousal* rather than love or hate. The fact is, the heroine from the romance stories may say she hates the hero, but she is spending all her time thinking about him, talking about him, and anticipating what he'll do next. In this sense, it almost doesn't matter that she finds him irritating!

The lesson here is that if passion, attraction, and chemistry are your goal, strong emotions are always preferable to limp, lukewarm agreement or indifference. An enormous study done by online dating giant OkCupid analyzed tons of data from their users and found something interesting—that the people who were most "polarizing" tended to be more successful overall. This means that those profiles that elicited strong feelings of both love and hate in people ended up working better than those straight-down-the-middle, inoffensive, and average profiles.

Intuitively, you'd assume that being average would mean you'd appeal to the widest range of people, but the truth is that you'd only ever elicit a lukewarm interest. Those people who risked sharing polarizing opinions (i.e., "love it or hate it") were more successful, because their approach allowed them to identify those people that were really, really into their unique quirks.

In other words, being "nice" is fine, but you may want to lead with weird, unique, or edgy instead. Boldly share those opinions that help sift out people—there will be some who will positively *hate* what you're sharing, but then again there will be others who will seriously love it. And this is likely to be more successful than merely trying to appeal to everyone by averaging out somewhere boring in the middle.

As an example, consider a slim, nerdy guy with lanky looks. He could try to compensate for this by bulking up, dressing like everyone else, and doing what he can to appeal to women who don't really like skinny guys. Or he could put his skinniness front and center.

He could dress to emphasize his thinness, play up his nerdy persona, and own it unabashedly, knowing that there are some women out there who go weak in the knees for it. His approach is polarizing—many (if not most) women will hate his look. But the few who don't? They'll be chasing him. And the only way he can identify those women is to broadcast his uniqueness loud and clear, not try to cover it up. It's a great way of looking at the "chase"—i.e., to completely narrow your focus and run in the race that you are already a winner in.

Takeaways:

- The chase is something we subconsciously do, despite outwardly decrying having to play dating games.
- Mostly, the chase has to do with the appeal and addictiveness of intermittent rewards and understanding why human nature works this way.
- The other portion of the chase is about how unavailability is attractive because we immediately begin to ruminate on what we are missing out on and what we are being deprived of.
- However, the chase is not a foolproof method, even though it takes advantage of

human psychology. Most of us have been faced with being rejected and told that we are only thought of as friends and not romantic partners. Is there a way to deal with this?

- For females, perhaps. Studies have shown that females do indeed see males platonically, but males do not do the same for females. Can males and females be only platonic friends? Yes, but it will usually be the female's choice.

- Finally, the deeper the love, the deeper the hate. Love and hate are closer than you think because they are both intense emotions. Work with love and hate in your own "chase" by leading with your polarizing attributes rather than aiming to please everyone in the boring middle.

Chapter 4. All About Flirting

Next time you have a free moment, stand outside an elementary school and watch the children play during recess. Make sure you're not wearing a trench coat and staring for too long; otherwise, the teachers will call the police on you.

While you're (surreptitiously) watching the children, take special note of how the little boys and girls interact. They will be flirting in the way only children do, and it will be pretty easy to spot. The boys will pick on the girls and pull their hair; the girls will scream and swat the boys away. The boys will throw soccer balls at the girls; the girls will keep the soccer balls and fold their arms together in sneers. Shins will get kicked, and cooties will be spread.

Adults do the exact same things, just in a subtler manner.

Flirting is the art of getting the attention of the opposite sex—what you use the attention for is up to you. Flirting is undeniably an important part of how we create attraction and get what we want romantically. It allows us to say, "Hey, I'm interested in you," without actually saying it, and sometimes the uncertainty makes the message even stronger.

Just as with any learned behavior, there are more and less effective ways of doing it as adults. Some of us are still stuck in the playground mentality of flirting that I just described. Others of us are flat-out trying to flirt incorrectly. I don't mean there is only one objectively correct way to flirt. Many people try to flirt in a way they have read about, but it isn't compatible with their personality or doesn't really work in the context of their lives. This obviously will lead to bad outcomes.

They try to be someone they're not, which completely takes away any advantage they may have had. It's like someone who's seven feet tall using the basketball strategies of someone who is five feet tall. The taller person may have read about the shorter person's strategies working, but they probably aren't a good fit for someone who can easily put the ball through the hoop by simply raising their hand.

There are specific types of flirting that work best for your personality and how you like to relate to the opposite sex. Take advantage of your unique strengths and quirks, and don't lose yourself trying to conform to what other people might advise you to do. It's a good idea to remember that successful flirting is all about two people feeling good in one another's company—if you're stressed out, running some cheesy script in your head, or unwittingly making the other person suspicious, uncomfortable, or anxious, then you're not really flirting anymore.

When two people *naturally* have chemistry, things seem to flow on their own. But that doesn't mean you can't learn to become better at creating the conditions that would allow that natural chemistry to flow more easily. You cannot force someone to be attracted to you, just as you cannot force yourself to be attracted to anyone you're not. But what you can do is grab their attention and play with them. You can make them laugh or smile, you can make them feel good and relaxed, and you can enjoy the interaction itself, regardless of where it goes and whether you consider it a success. (Tip: for a woman, nothing makes a man seem more desperate and unappealing than the sense that he is talking to her because and only because he wants to sleep with her.)

The Stages of Flirting

When was the last time you were out at a bar or club at closing time?

If you were sober and took a look around, you might have observed some very interesting aspects of human mating. This is the stage of the night when people want to seal the deal and move from the bar to someone's bed. Here, we see the mechanisms of the dating game stripped to their barest. More desperate measures are taken, and we can see the mechanics of attraction play out more clearly than perhaps anywhere else. We can also see that some people are consistently successful, while others almost always go home alone.

Why is that? Is it really just that some of us are that much more charming, or is there something going on in the background they have tapped into?

One scientifically proven answer lies within *scripts*. People follow scripts for pretty much everything they engage in, from ordering at a restaurant to going to the doctor's office.

For example, at Burger King, you know someone is going to ask for your order, ask if you want a drink with it, and then you will pay them. After you pay them, you will get a receipt and then be pointed to an area where you wait for your food. That's just one of many scripts we know and are familiar with in our daily lives. It means that you know exactly how to act in that situation, you know what to expect, you know what stage you're at, and you know what you're missing. It allows you to consistently be successful there. Waiting for the cashier to give you the receipt and your order number is almost instinctual. You don't think about it because it's a script you've engaged in countless times.

It shouldn't be a surprise, then, that going from strangers to flirting to the possibility of sex has a script as well, a script that makes it easy to escalate from one stage to the next because of how familiar it all seems. It's just not a script that we have known explicitly, until 1980 when Timothy Perper and Susan

Fox studied and determined the exact stages of successful flirtation to sex.

Knowing this script is more important than you might think. Just as you know the script for success at Burger King, knowing the script that Perper and Fox discovered will show you methods for successful flirting, period. You will be able to see what you are missing, what you may have skipped, what you still need to do, and, overall, how to achieve your goal of sex via flirting. You should also integrate this knowledge with the previous section's discovery of your flirting style to see how you might be falling short.

The researchers sat in singles bars and watched people who entered alone and ended up leaving with other people at the end of the night. In other words, these were people who started as strangers, then utilized flirting as a means to sex. They discovered three main stages in the script for successful flirtation of those who more often than not left with someone for the night. Those who weren't successfully typically ended the interaction early on, or else tried to change the order of the stages.

The stages are:

1. Approach
2. Synchronize
3. Touch

We'll go through each in more detail so you can see exactly what's involved in a successful flirtation interaction, no matter the style of flirting.

The first stage is the approach stage. As you might guess, this governs how a successful approach of a stranger for flirtation works. If the approach is not received warmly or at all, the flirtation will immediately end. Now, this isn't to say that a perfect approach will necessarily succeed every time—there are two people in every social interaction, and if one of them doesn't want to play, there is simply no game. Nevertheless, we can do a lot on our side of the bargain to broach that distance gracefully and approach another person in a way that leads to a positive outcome.

So what is involved in a successful approach? The researchers articulated three distinct points that would predict how well an approach would go.

The first factor was the direction and orientation of the approach. Males disliked being approached from the front, but females disliked being approached from the side (Fisher & Byrne, 1975). This speaks to how the different genders felt about violations of personal space. Males felt more comfortable being approached from the side, whereas females felt more comfortable being approached from the front. This means females actually felt more comfortable with a greater degree of violation of their personal space. Males tended to welcome directness, while females wanted to first feel more secure and less threatened. Choose the wrong orientation and the first stage is set up for failure.

The second factor is smiles. The researchers found that the more each party smiled, the more a successful approach was likely to have occurred. It didn't matter whether the participants approached with a joke or even a serious conversation topic. The smile indicated an emotional arousal, interest on a party's behalf, and the willingness to show that interest to the other person. Of note, only genuine smiles were indicative; an insincere smile was characterized by being delayed, a lack of eye wrinkles, and a lack of teeth shown.

The final factor that determined a successful

approach was people's use of their eyebrows and overall facial expressiveness. When we use our eyebrows separately and independently from other nonverbal gestures, we are essentially conveying interest with them. The researchers called this "flashing" our eyebrows. Using eyebrow flashes was more successful when approaching the opposite sex and led to people being able to continue along the script.

Synchronization. This is the second stage to a successful flirtation interaction and will only occur when the first stage of approaching was successful. Of course, the script is sequential because the so-called prospect must feel additional levels of warmth and comfort in order for the end goal to come to fruition.

This is important, and a big reason that flirting can flop or leave the other person cold. Some men approach a woman so focused on the desired outcome that they tend to rush the process or speed along at a pace that isn't reciprocated. You may have researched the script in your mind all night, but she has only seen you for all of five seconds and suddenly you're in her space and talking to her at a thousand miles an hour!

If the other person is giving you any signal at all that your approach has not been successful, then trying to push on to synchronization is likely to make things worse. They'll only feel like you're being rude and pushy. Only once the actual physical approach is accepted or welcomed, then a conversation can begin.

Other various studies have expounded on what types of pickup lines work best. The ones that worked best in the flirtation context were not cute and flippant. Trying too hard to be clever had a higher chance of failure. What worked more consistently, and was reported to generate higher levels of interest, were simple, straightforward introductions or observations about the environment. In other words, keep it simple, stupid. An effective pickup line, or some kind of conversation starter, is important because it's what leads to quick synchronization.

The reason this stage is called "synchronize" is because people's bodies will literally synchronize to face each other, and their movements and energy will become similar so as to adjust and adapt to the other person. That's what happens when you participate in an engaging conversation with someone you

118

hold in high regard. When rapport and interest are established, we begin mirroring their tone of voice and body language in an effort to appear more similar, and thus attractive, to them.

A successful synchronization stage is characterized by people simply looking directly at each other, making eye contact, being physically close, and appearing engaged. Both parties have signaled that they are interested in a continuing interaction by locking their positions. Initial attraction has been built, and they pass each other's superficial filters and first impressions. They're speaking, but they're also analyzing each other's body language and facial expressions to determine the level of interest they should show.

This is where the flirtation game truly begins—it's a subtle test of how attracted you really are to the other person. After physical synchronization, physical touch begins.

Touch. At this point, both physical and mental attraction has been established, and it's time to escalate. This is the final stage of a successful flirtation interaction: if the parties successfully touch each other, and the touch is received warmly, then the feedback will spur the parties to touch each other more, and the rest is history.

Remember again that the previous stage needs to be properly established before moving on to the next. If you are trying to synchronize with someone and for whatever reasons it's just not happening, don't think that you can hurry things along by using touch—this will probably only make the lack of synchronicity more obvious.

Of course, this stage isn't only about touch. It's about the continued rapport and tension that is created as a result of being in close proximity with each other. Touching heightens that and makes intentions clearer. Both parties will start at more neutral touching that can be interpreted in multiple ways before diving into the types of touch that are unmistakable in their intent and purpose. Breaking the touch barrier can feel electric.

If the touch barrier has been crossed and accepted by both parties, the script comes to an end because there is nowhere else to escalate to—in public, at least. You might differ on the path you took to get here, but this script was observed to be highly effective. The three stages of flirting that

Perper and Fox found aren't a guarantee of sex, but if you make sure to hit these stages, you will set yourself up for success.

Now that we know the stages of flirting to sex, what should we do with this knowledge? We need to diagnose how we send out our own messages, what we are doing, and what we aren't doing.

For example, many people think they make their intentions well known, but they never so much as touch their intended mates. Clearly, that's something to address because they are not following the flirting script that has been proven to be effective and successful.

Others may skip right over the approach phase and immediately begin touching. That's too aggressive and forward for most people. What the script actually defines is the process of building rapport and comfort with strangers. Turns out it functions the same at networking events as it does for flirting and sex.

This script is highly simplified, but that's about as good as you can get for human interaction. There are so many shades of gray and different interpretations of the same action that three steps are as good of a guideline as you are going to get.

This allows us to visualize what we should be doing or what we should be looking for. If you want to approach a stranger, you should make sure that your actual physical approach is improved and smooth and that you have a conversation starter immediately ready to employ. Then, after building rapport with humor, you should begin touching to create a sense of tension and attraction. Don't skip ahead, and don't neglect a step thinking that you are above it or don't need it. It's been scientifically proven that you're not so special that you don't!

If some of this sounds clinical, it's because to some degree, it is. Humans study the behavior of rats by adjusting variables and administering more cheese or shocks. Human patterns of behavior can be studied in essentially the same way. However, when done "in the wild" and naturally, you'll find that people tend to follow this formula whether they know it or not. The sex drive is one of the most powerful human motivators, and in a sense, can make us predictable sometimes. Flirting is to running through mazes, and the possibility of sex is to cheese if you were to continue along that analogy.

Understand your flirting style and then understand how it fits, or doesn't fit, into the stages of flirting that have been observed to work. And no kicking of shins.

A Word on First Impressions—and Walking the Walk

Okay, so we know it's good to approach women from the front and men from the side, and it's good to smile, and it's good to use your facial expressions strategically during the "approach" part of the flirting process. However, there's a factor you might not have considered when it comes to approaching a new person for the first time: the way you walk. Fascinating research is continually uncovering all the tiny bits of data people perceive (even unconsciously) and analyze in a split second to make a judgment about the people in front of them.

If you've ever secretly wondered whether pickup lines make absolutely no difference, well, you may be right. Some studies have found that even *before* you approach someone, they are able to generate lasting first impressions about the kind of person you are—and people may make snap decisions long before you even open your mouth. These automatic assessments are made on such tiny amounts of data that even a single photograph has most people making personality judgments.

Yes, our facial expression, accent, voice, and the words we're saying are all important, but the way we carry our bodies in space is in many ways the most easily observable trait—especially from a distance. If you've ever seen someone in a bar make an approach to someone and be instantly shut down even before they say a word, you can be sure it had something to do with the literal walk on the way over. It doesn't seem entirely fair to make such a snap judgment on gait alone, but remember that this is the power of intuition and animal impulse—it's fast and it's decisive, and there's no arguing with it!

A 2012 study in the journal *Cognition* published findings that suggest that people can make pretty quick judgments about others based on an astonishingly small amount of visual data and "motion components." Based on very tiny perceptions of the way a body moves—for example, through style of walking (or gait)—people were able to form impressions about a stranger's personality traits.

A 2019 study by Fink et. al. in *Biology Letters* explains how women are able to accurately assess a man's physical strength by watching his gait, with strong walkers assessed as more attractive—however, this is not universal and varies depending on culture. Another study by Nicolas Guéguen in the journal *Gait and Posture* explored how women who are ovulating (and therefore more fertile) may unconsciously walk more slowly and in a way that observers rate as sexier. First impressions about who you are can greatly impact how attractive you seem to others—so it would be wise to make sure you're making the best first impression possible!

How do you do that? First of all, it's important to remember that many of these judgments have evolved over millions of years and are for the most part unconscious, intuitive and automatic. We're talking about snap decisions about another person's sexual fitness based on very primal perceptions, here. In other words, you can't really fake it.

Have you ever heard people say something like, "I get that he/she is good looking, but they do absolutely nothing for me"? That's because when people assess you on a biological level, any rational or cultural assessments don't really matter—either the chemistry is there or it isn't.

If you want to improve how you come across to the opposite sex, focus on how your *entire body* is presented. An upright posture usually signals to people that you are confident and self-assured, because people who are comfortable in themselves hold themselves (literally) in high regard. But if you adopt an upright posture, you can convince others and yourself that you are more confident than you perhaps feel. Standing up straight will help, but at the same time consider all the ways you can boost your confidence so that you are naturally standing taller—doing so will mean you are not acting like someone who is attractive, you *are* someone who is attractive.

Similarly, be mindful of how you walk and hold yourself in space. Don't rush or fidget, and be aware of tensions in your muscles. Before you socialize or have a conversation, take a moment to consciously relax and release your breath, drop your shoulders, lift your chin, and relax your jaw. People who are calm and sure of themselves are automatically more attractive.

Finally, be more aware of not just your

posture, but how you move in space. The best way to have more physical presence? Exercise. Being strong, healthy, and fit from within will broadcast to others (even if only on an unconscious level) that you are capable, disciplined, healthy, and vibrant. If you are comfortable in your skin, it shows.

If you have difficulty with being awkward or clumsy, you may find that practicing any dance form or even a martial art will help you strengthen your mind-body connection, and the small changes this makes to your physiology will be noticeable to others. Try yoga, calisthenics, sports, or anything that gets your body feeling strong and healthy. Then, you'll find yourself naturally more "embodied," more confident and more at ease in yourself. Even if you never say a word, you can communicate to others that you may be disconnected from your body, uncomfortable with yourself, or unhealthy in some way. Relationships and dating come down to sex and sexual attractiveness, and that comes down to what bodies think of other bodies. The best way to make a first impression is to think carefully—what message might your body be sending long before you open your mouth to speak?

The Friendship Formula and How to Use It

Dr. Jack Schafer is a retired FBI agent who once worked on the National Security Behavioral Analysis Program. What does he have to do with becoming a better flirt? Well, according to Schafer, people tend to like one another and classify one another as friends when four specific aspects are in place. The "friendship formula" goes like this:

Friendship = Proximity + Frequency + Duration + Intensity.

Let's break it down to see what he meant. We're all going about our lives constantly scanning the environment and the people in it, deciding, consciously or unconsciously, who is friend or foe and who to approach or avoid. We tend to make this appraisal based on the above four factors.

Proximity means how close you are to someone. This can mean physical proximity (i.e., you share a house with a roommate and you see them every day) or it can mean contextual closeness or simply feeling that a person is always "there" somehow. Frequency is how often you encounter one another. In school, where you met with your friends every single weekday and probably

128

on the weekends too, you might have formed friendships ultra-quickly, whereas your friendships took ages to get off the ground since you had to make do with meeting up once every few weeks or months.

INSTANT DATE

Duration matters, too—longer interactions tend to create more familiarity and friendship feelings than fleeting ones. Finally, intensity is about the degree to which you satisfy the other person's needs by spending time with them. This really depends on the kind of interaction, the people involved, and the needs in question. If you've ever complained of missing out on quality time with your partner or get bored with shallow friends, you might have experienced low intensity, i.e., your needs for connection were not really being met.

So, what does all of this mean for the flirting game?

The above four aspects are naturally found when people are in that warm fuzzy getting-to-know-you phase, but you can engineer those positive feelings yourself. If you're aware of the fact that people are always scanning their environment to judge people friend or foe, and you know how they're making those judgments, then you can position yourself strategically.

Step 1: Start with proximity. If you're interested in someone as a friend or more, just begin by being around them more. Importantly, don't begin with increasing intensity—someone who is coming on strong from out of the blue is likely to be perceived only as a threat or irritation. Don't be pushy or weird about it, but keep things light and casual. Simply try to figure out ways you can naturally and comfortably be around them more. Establish yourself as part of the furniture, basically.

Step 2: Now you can increase the duration and frequency of interactions. Take it slow and don't barge ahead with some idea of how the interaction should go, but take your cue from the other person.

Step 3: Only once you're regularly interacting with this person should you attempt to dial up the intensity. This is where interactions cross over into friendship and deeper connections. Here, you start to really understand one another, and your interactions prove mutually beneficial, i.e., you both find your respective needs satisfied.

The flirting formula of approach, synchronize,

and touch works better for short-term interactions—like when you're in a bar or on a promising first date. In these contexts, there is already the shared understanding that romantic possibility exists, so people are likely to be receptive to you making a move. However, many people have learned the hard way that trying some of these techniques in the wrong context is liable to get pretty embarrassing results. Randomly flirting with people while they're at the store, at work or on the street? Hopefully the friendship formula shows you why diving in with intensity right off the bat will probably only lead to defensiveness or a flat out rejection.

Use the three-step flirting process if you have some reason to believe the other person will be open and receptive to it—for example, they're in a noisy club, on a dating app, or have indeed made the first move themselves. Use the flirting process if you don't have much time and want to make a connection quickly, based primarily on catching attention and building attraction.

Use the friendship formula if you're looking for more than a hookup and want to build the foundations of what could become a genuine relationship. You could gradually ramp up proximity, frequency, duration, and intensity, and then seal the deal by flirting. Whatever your approach, though, remember that when you're closing the distance between you and someone you're interested in, a few golden rules always apply:

- Go step by step and build a connection gradually (if not, you may be perceived as threatening, disrespectful, or too intense)
- Note how you're being received and adjust accordingly (if not, you can come across as selfish or unempathetic)

Takeaways:

- Flirting is hard to define, but in general, the goal is to gain someone's attention and make it known that you are interested in them. There are many ways to do this, but not everything will work for everyone.
- Researchers have additionally discovered a three-step process people who were successful in leaving with someone from bars used consistently. The three steps are approach, synchronize, and touch. It's important to analyze what you are doing,

what you are not doing, and if you are skipping over a step or staying on one too long. You should also consider how your flirting style fits into this process.

- This approach is best used in situations where you have reason to believe the other person is receptive to them.
- Dr. Jack Schafer's friendship formula states that people build connections when they are in proximity to one another, when their interactions are frequent and long in duration, and when both parties get their needs met.
- Schafer's theory can be applied to flirting, especially in contexts where the three-part flirting process wouldn't be appropriate.
- Whichever approach you use (short-term flirting or longer-term connection-building) remember top go step by step, building gradually on pervious connection, and adjust your approach carefully based on how you're being received.

Chapter 5. Love Is All That Matters . . .

Arranged marriages are a spin on love that hasn't quite made the jump to the so-called Western world. To most people in Western cultures, the notion fundamentally redefines the entire purpose of marriage in a less than positive way.

In the West, marriage is about freedom, choice, and, ultimately, love. An arranged marriage, at least from a superficial standpoint, involves values that are the mirror opposite of liberty and diversity of options. Love is entirely about emotional connection and chemistry, so how can you reduce it to an arrangement where the participants don't even meet each other until weeks or days before their wedding?

When parents in traditional Asian cultures, Indian in particular, arrange marriages for their children, they factor in compatibility and long-term prospects and tend to assume that physical attractiveness or love are less important, if they matter at all. It will better inform the rest of this chapter if we first take a look at how the Indian matchmaking and arranged marriage process works. I took it upon myself to perform due diligence and survey over a dozen Indian couples who had arranged marriages, as well as an Indian matchmaker. Bear with me—the results say a lot about marriage and love in general.

Arranged Marriages and What We Can Learn From Them

Let's take two single individuals, Neha and Kunal, who live in Mumbai, India.

They are both nearing twenty-six years old, and their parents decide they now need to take charge and help their children start their own families. It's a decision their parents and family make, because that's exactly who tends to take the lead in securing spouses for their children. In many cases, young Indian adults rely entirely on their parents and family for this part of their life and only make fledgling attempts at romance themselves before they begin the process with their parents.

Indian arranged marriages are approached by the parents and families like a business decision first and foremost. Both sets of parents will shine a beacon into the community and ask their friends and acquaintances if they know anyone suitable for their child, all the while selling their virtues like a beautiful piece of pottery.

Neha's and Kunal's parents have a mutual friend with whom they attended university, and that friend has made both sets of parents aware that there was a single young adult of the opposite sex who seemed like a good match on paper. That is, they were close in age, their families had similar standing and finances, and, most important, Neha and Kunal were both sufficiently acceptable (if not impressive) to the other person's parents. In essence, we're talking about a matchmaker.

The parents were put in touch, details were ironed out and confirmed, and then pictures were sent along for approval to Neha's and Kunal's families. Kunal was a bit more enthused than Neha by the pictures, but both agreed to meet the following week.

Neha and Kunal met at a café for about two hours, but it probably didn't resemble any date you've been on. Their meeting was fairly serious and more like a discussion about whether a business partnership would be appropriate. They discussed long-term goals, values, shared morals, and questions designed to determine how they felt about certain issues. They ended the date with a handshake and went home with their parents to discuss how it went.

If the "date" and the post-date discussion with their parents went extremely well, the couple might not even meet again before agreeing to marry and notifying each other of their intent. Because the truly important factors that determine compatibility and fit (though not love) are discussed honestly and openly, combined with an extremely high degree of commitment, the marriage is deemed to have an extremely high chance of success. As you can see, nowhere in the description of that process was affection even mentioned. If they happened to have some chemistry, that would be icing on the cake, but it's not seen as a prerequisite to marriage.

But what about love?

What is love's role in arranged marriage? Love marriages, as they are referred to in India, are driven by connection and chemistry while family, values, and lifestyle are often drowned out and completely ignored. Arranged marriages on the other hand go in the reverse direction—they are driven by the logical, practical, and financial side of things, and once those are in place, fondness and affection are assumed to grow.

Phrased in this light, it's almost too easy to see why there are so many bumps in Western marriages, and that the current (2017) rate of divorce is roughly thirty percent according to data from the National Survey of Family Growth. The Western idea of compatibility has long been confined to elusive chemistry, with total disregard for practicality.

It's not taken into account per se, but the belief is that once the big factors involving values and worldviews are accounted for, love that starts with familiarity will take care of itself and slowly evolve. For the matchmakers, love is seen as something that grows over time as a function of a few things.

This could be explained by the *proximity effect*, which is a psychological phenomenon in which people who share the same proximity tend to like each other more and more with time. There have been studies conducted in which subjects rated people more favorably merely because they spent more time with them or because they had been physically closer to them. It's why we have a certain type of affection for our neighbors, the baristas we see every morning, or the odd person on the bus you see weekly. Familiarity, then, doesn't always breed contempt, but rather comfort.

With the proximity effect, arranged marriages find suitable matches in every respect minus love, and love and affection can then grow between any two people living and working together in close proximity.

Another thing to consider is that people who consent to arranged unions also place a high premium on commitment. This plays a tremendous role in how well the marriage fares in the future. Francine Kaye, a relationship and marriage expert, had this to say on commitment in arranged marriages:

> *It should be pointed out that arranged marriages work because culturally marriage is seen differently. We have a very romantic view of marriage. Theirs*

is more pragmatic . . . In the West, marriages are easy to get out of. But in arranged marriages, the commitment is very strong. They get married knowing they won't leave, so when times are harder—if they face injury or trauma— they don't run away. It brings them closer.

When a partner looks at the marriage more like a partnership or business relationship, they put more focus into making it work. They don't see leaving or divorce as an option and are thus committed to solving issues and compromise. Having disagreements or lacking that spark are not seen as legitimate reasons to end a relationship, whereas they may be the nail in the coffin for love marriages built on attraction and love alone. This tendency to look into the future and get around problems before they appear gives arranged marriages a strategic advantage that passion-based relationships do not have.

You're solving problems with solutions that should last fifty years, so what actions will you take to make it work? It's going to be significantly different. People who get into arranged marriages do not look at passion or any short-term consideration. Rather, they look at whether they are going to have children, the quality of the education of those children, and other factors that look way into the future. They also look at retirement and growing old together.

There is an emphasis on problem-solving and conflict skills, which studies have also confirmed is a primary indicator of marriage longevity and happiness. The parents, who are older and have experienced marriage themselves, step in and offer their wisdom, and the family in general weigh in on a match and its attributes that go far beyond the couple themselves.

Marriages, despite what some people might present to the outside world, are never conflict-free lovefests. Even with the best of friends and lovers, there are bound to be fights. When you spend most of your day with someone, logic dictates that you don't agree one hundred percent on everything. In fact, you can look at it this way: if you agree on eighty percent of matters, that's just a rounding error from one hundred percent because one hundred percent doesn't exist.

So when you hit a bump in the road, do you handle it or sweep it under the rug? If you sweep it under the rug, it will fester and leak out in the form of passive-aggressive behavior before turning into full-out bitterness and resentment? If you choose to address it, are you doing so in a way that will lead to a solution and not further entrenchment?

More successful and happy couples have open lines of communication. They can more easily deal with such issues in a productive manner because they don't overreact or inject emotion into the issue. Their focus on commitment makes them focus on being solution-oriented. If you imagine that your marriage is indeed forever and for life, then you might as well attempt to find a solution as soon as possible instead of suffering with your problem for decades.

On a related note, there's the simple expectation that it's going to take work. Nothing will be easy, and you can't simply sweep it under the rug. If you barely know someone, you know you will need to invest considerable effort, and this is the type of effort most "love" marriages don't have—because they don't necessarily see the need to. It's amazing the difference expectations can make.

It may sound unromantic and clinical, but a series of studies by Harvard's Dr. Robert

Epstein led him to conclude, based on a series of tests on romantic love and passion developed by Elaine Hatfield and Susan Sprecher, that feelings of passionate and romantic love are only at about half-capacity after eighteen months in a relationship. It's not unreasonable to project that after three or four years, those feelings are considerably more withered.

Meanwhile, love in arranged marriages appears to grow gradually and linearly and actually surpasses the levels of love in love marriages at about the five-year point. He also found that after ten years together, the affection in arranged marriages is twice as strong as that in love marriages—because of the matching values and similarities.

Additional studies were conducted at the University of Rajasthan with the same conclusion. Love marriages under one year old averaged a score of seventy out of ninety-one on a love scale, and the numbers fell consistently over time. After ten years, they had an average score of forty. Arranged marriages under one year old averaged a score of fifty-eight out of ninety-one. Yet, after ten years, they scored an average of sixty-eight. Arranged marriages might start lower, but on a long-term basis, they might indeed produce happier and healthier marriages.

It's not a stretch to say that compatibility is about much more than chemistry and connection, both of which are destined to fade. The message underlying these differences with arranged marriages is that attraction comes as a byproduct of commitment, proximity, and problem-solving. It sounds a bit more like a relationship with coworkers.

And love marriages? Well, Epstein sums it up well:

> *The idea is we must not leave our love lives to chance. We plan our education, our careers, and our finances, but we're still uncomfortable with the idea that we should plan our love lives. I do not advocate arranged marriages, but I think a lot can be learned from them.*

It's not the fairytale that we've been sold since our childhood, but since when has that been realistic? I'm not sure I see Cinderellas and Snow Whites roaming around the streets.

So what does all this mean for you? Returning to the four sequential steps of attraction we covered way back in the first chapter, we can see that the Western model begins with attraction and then uses that to fuel the journey to commitment and logical relationship building based on shared values. The Indian approach goes the other direction and starts with the logical and practical considerations first, laying them down and hoping that this will in turn kindle the other steps in attraction. Historically, many cultures have seen raw, unbridled physical passion as something that simply has nothing to do with marriage—it's nice, but it's flimsy and fleeting and no basis for a long-term relationship.

When you're mating and dating, focus on how you two fit together in a business sense, just like the Indian process emphasizes. Even if you value physical compatibility and basic attraction, most people also want long-term security and commitment, and this requires consideration for things beyond immediate attraction. Everyone likes to be able to see the long-term view and how everything will work out years down the road, so if you can make that more salient and obvious (to yourself and your potential partners), you will be tackling the issue with open eyes.

Arranged marriages are often accused of

being unromantic or downplaying love. Nothing could be further from the truth; the difference is in the role love plays and the position it occupies in the grand scheme. Arranged marriages see love as a flower that grows in time from a tree that is carefully and painstakingly planted in the right soil. Love marriages can be this too, but often they are the equivalent of finding a lovely wildflower and expecting it to grow into an enormous strong tree when you take it home and put it in the ground. It may, and it may not.

What should your approach be? This comes down to your values and preferences. It's about your perspective and your timescale. What are you seeking in a mate—not just right now but in the future? If, like most people, you want a long-term partner that you can build a happy life with, you need to see attraction as just one part of the puzzle, and not the most important part. If you're a romantic at heart, well . . . follow your heart! Just know that some romance stories are beautiful precisely because they are ephemeral and insubstantial. Have you noticed how the fairy stories end with "and they lived happily ever after" but you never hear the details of that living? That's because even the grandest love stories look very different after ten years, three kids, two house moves, and several life tragedies. "Love" doesn't matter at that point—commitment, communication, and shared values, however, do.

The Triangular Theory of Love

Let's be a bit more concrete about what we're saying when it comes to love, commitment and plain physical attraction. Answering the question "what is love?" is a little tricky, but we can identify different *kinds* of love, or at least what loves looks like in different stages. Robert Sternberg is a psychologist who founded a theory of interpersonal relationships that he called the Triangular Theory of Love. He believed that relationships could play out along three distinct scales:

Intimacy
Passion
Commitment

The problem many people have with arranged marriages is obvious: the commitment and intimacy are there, but the passion can be lacking. With Western-style love marriages, the trouble is that there can be buckets of passion and intimacy, but difficulty around commitment. For Sternberg, a successful relationship is inevitably one that scores highly on as many of these scales as possible—i.e., one that is moderately intimate, passionate, and committed is likely to be stronger than one that scores highly in only one or two areas.

Yes, the relative weight of each different aspect may change according to life stage and indeed individual difference and preference. But Sternberg found the best relationships were those that had enough of all three.

Let's look more closely:
Passion is all about physical attraction, sex, "chemistry," and that delightful spark that surrounds all forms of flirting and romance. **Intimacy** is general emotional closeness, feeling connected and bonded in love to the other person. Finally, **commitment** is a more active decision about how you will behave in the long term—i.e., to cultivate and nurture that love. It's as though passion is the first fiery spark or lightning bolt, intimacy is the warm softly glowing fire that results, and commitment is the active decision, over time, to keep giving fuel to that fire to sustain it.

So far, so good. How can we use this theory in our own love lives, though?

Well, good relationships are those that possess as much of each metric as possible, but it's also a question of overlap and compatibility. To illustrate, imagine that every person's involvement in a relationship is represented by a triangle. If they experience a high degree of attraction and a lot of intimacy and feel committed, they can be represented by a nice full and balanced equilateral triangle. However, imagine another person who is high on intimacy and passion but low on commitment, so they're a more lopsided triangle.

Overlay these two triangles on top of each other—the degree to which they don't overlap represents tension and difficulty. In relationship, these two people may butt heads over the issue of commitment. Their problem will be different from another couple, though, who, for example, have the same broad shape triangle, only one is much bigger than the other—this couple is likely to have one partner feeling more emotionally invested and in love than the other.

Fundamentally, every couple will have their own unique struggles, but Sternberg's theory shows that ultimately these struggles come down to three broad areas of what we call love, as well as a mismatch between where each partner is on that scale.

Arranged marriages can be very successful.
Love marriages can be very successful.
Yet each has a different strategy for finding and maintaining "love."
Sternberg would say that neither approach is necessarily better, but that truly successful partnerships have a balanced and matched combination of attraction, commitment, and intimacy.

In an arranged marriage where intimacy and commitment are high, the couple may nevertheless completely lack passion and work together more as a platonic team raising children and managing a domestic life. This setup can work, but it's naturally going to be less resilient than one that has the intimacy and commitment *and* a rock-solid sex life!

When you are dating someone new, you might be tempted to rate them on only one scale or maybe two—attraction and intimacy. But a relationship based on this alone is less likely to survive long term. Ask yourself:

What does my "love triangle" look like?
What does my partner's look like?
How do we compare and overlap?

What could we do to offset and improve on some of our weaker areas?

This last question is interesting. Some people would say that the most important aspect of the above three is physical attraction, since it's the only one that can't be faked or summoned up by will alone, whereas the other two are conscious choices that are easier to control. On the other hand, there's no guarantee that consciously nailing down commitment and intimacy will allow attraction to flourish—otherwise, all friendships would tend toward romance with time, and that isn't the case.

At any rate, breaking down the love experience into these three categories can give you insight and help you talk about the vague and difficult to measure "love" in a more concrete and useful way. When you say you're in love with someone, what do you mean? What do they mean? How do those perspectives line up with one another? Getting a clearer picture on these questions may spell the difference between a failed relationship and a mutually satisfying one.

Love or Similarity?

We've taken a look at how love can take a back seat to problem-solving skills and a simple commitment to work and investment. Here's another proposition: love may also be less important than how *similar* you are to your potential mate.

Would you want to date someone with the same traits and interests as you, or someone who is different but *complementary*?

It's one of the questions we've asked ourselves multiple times without even realizing it. When we meet someone new, we instinctively wonder how we'll fit together. Is it going to be two identical puzzle pieces, or are you going to be two puzzle pieces that fit together to complete the picture? Do you need someone that thinks in the exact same way as you, or do you need someone who complements your weaknesses and balances you out?

Conventional wisdom (something that people repeat enough so that it seems that it should be true) dictates that opposites attract. And at first glance, there is wisdom in this idea. Opposites can smooth each other's flaws and make each other stronger in areas where they are weak. We admire people who can do things we cannot, so naturally we like our opposites at times. The whole is stronger than the sum of its parts.

Opposites can be complementary to us and introduce us to an entirely different world. It can be a thrilling challenge and take us outside of our comfort zones to grow as people. Things are novel and exciting every day. Besides, when you've just started dating someone, the honeymoon period effect is fairly strong and you overlook most things. Who's to say that initially you would pay attention to how similar or different you two are?

The thing you might find adorable and endearing just might be the same thing that drives you up the wall after the honeymoon period. So what happens after the relationship is past that glorious honeymoon period? This is where conventional wisdom hits some rough spots. When the novelty dies, you're left with two people who share completely different values.

There is a reason why, in survey after survey, successful couples in long-term relationships tend to be flat-out similar (Kaufman, 2011). Studies have even shown that couples that *look more alike* physically tend to be happier and in longer relationships.

Many people make the mistake of believing that their dissimilar interests and values will intertwine at some point. This is essentially the belief that you or your partner will fundamentally change. For example, that the other person will change or that you will eventually be able to change their minds about foundational beliefs that are tied to their identity. How many marriages have ended over the fact that one party wanted children, the other didn't, and both thought the other would eventually change?

How many people have wished for their partner to convert religions or political positions for them but are upset when neither party wishes to change? When both parties believe the other person will change, it means they themselves aren't willing to, and the chance of a compromise is even lower. Values don't change as a result of osmosis or proximity. They're deep-seated and, even with effort, can't easily change. The same goes for interests.

According to the studies, truly successful couples tended to have similar interests when their relationship started, and they bonded over their similarity. They liked to do similar things and shared similar views on important issues.

Their similarity may even have been the impetus for their relationship beginning because it caused one of the parties to lower their guard and be open to the other. There's a fairly strong evolutionary basis for preferring similarity. We were more likely to survive if we stuck to shapes, shadows, and sounds we recognized versus unfamiliar ones that could be saber-toothed tigers lurking in the shadows.

There's also a very human element to similarity. What if you met someone and you discovered that you grew up just minutes away from each other in the same tiny town in another country? You're going to automatically see them in another light and be more open to them, and this can be the beginning of a romantic relationship.

So opposites do *attract*, but to finish the quote, opposites then *attack*. The factors that set you apart will eventually bubble to the surface. We have to tackle the inconvenient reality that pairings involving opposite personalities tend to break up more frequently (Hudson & Fraley, 2014).

Let's indulge in stereotypes.

An artisan performer can be drawn to a rational banker and vice versa. The banker can be drawn to the performer because the performer is socially driven, gregarious, loves to live loudly, and is very optimistic. The performer can be drawn to the banker because they are organized, cautious, fun to make fun of, and a realist.

These differences in temperament, which are polar opposites, help complete both personalities. Both parties feel they are more complete individuals within the relationship. But the seeds of destruction have also been planted.

The rational banker is very big on money management and personal responsibility. The artisan, on the other hand, is not very good with money or time management. The banker's cold personality orientation can lead to the artisan feeling shut out and as if defensive walls are up. The artisan is extremely spontaneous and carefree, while the banker must plan things days in advance (and not only because their job has long and demanding hours).

Sooner or later, that relationship will go on life support, sustaining it long after it should have naturally ended. The culprits here are the deep and fundamental differences in the personality orientations of the partners.

Both partners need to be honest regarding their own needs and those of their partner's—sometimes you just can't fulfill them because you are too different. Usually, people don't change for others. They are mostly incapable of it, and that's okay. The best they can do is alter their behavior to appease their significant other. And although that is important, it's also ephemeral and therefore temporary—though not for lack of trying or absence of desire to accommodate.

A lot of heartache and fertile years could be saved if we internalized this fact of life. People usually can't or don't change who they are at their core. We all want to be the exception to the rule, but that's statistically just not reasonable or possible.

What does this mean for your relationship? You have to try to suss out whether someone is really trying to change or just appeasing you with token actions. The former is a far stronger motivation, but unfortunately it's not easy for people themselves to tell what is driving them—a desire to change or a desire to avoid negative consequences from you.

In a study on whether couples that were more similar in personality were happier than couples that were less similar, subjects rated their own personalities while their partners did the same. They rated their personality based on five metrics, which are generally known as the "big five" of personality traits based on additional studies.

The traits are:

1. Extraversion: how much engagement with the outside world is preferred
2. Conscientiousness: how structured and disciplined one is
3. Openness: willingness to do things that are novel, new, and out of their comfort zone
4. Agreeableness: empathy, trust, and consideration for others
5. Emotional stability (or neuroticism): the ability to be emotionally unreactive and able to cope with negativity

After they rated their personalities, they also completed a questionnaire assessing how happy they were in their current relationship. The results were surprising given the thrust of this chapter.

Of the five personality factors, there were only two that mattered in relationship satisfaction: *agreeableness* and *emotional stability*. The other three factors, extraversion, conscientiousness, and openness, did not need to be similar for a happy relationship.

This might not be surprising if you consider that agreeableness and emotional stability are the two personality factors that could plausibly define compromise and how you might gracefully disagree and have arguments. The other three factors don't take others into account.

Love matters. Or does it? Is it a social construct that has been sold to us via romantic comedies and Disney movies with dashing princes? Or is it something that is the subject of misplaced hopes and dreams?

Takeaways:

- Love is what most of us marry for, but arranged marriages have been around for a very long time. In fact, what most of us would consider romantic love is a luxury that is only a few hundred years old.
- Arranged marriages work precisely because love is placed as a low priority.

Instead, commitment, problem-solving, and lowered expectations take the forefront and create conditions that allow for a harmonious relationship to first blossom, which allows love to follow.

- Another factor that appears to be more important than love in relationships is similarity. Studies have shown that similarity is more important because people don't tend to change, and over time, you're just left with conflicting values and worldviews.

- The triangular theory of love states that the most successful relationships score well on all three metrics: attraction, intimacy, and commitment. Happy couples need to have strong overlap and match in their "triangles" or else work to strengthen their weak points.

- A study specified the traits that predicted the most relationship success if similar: agreeableness and emotional stability. Conventional wisdom says that opposites attract, but for successful long-term partnerships, shared values and similarity in interest, communication, preferences, etc. are usually more valuable.

Chapter 6. How to Know What You Want (You Don't)

So, we've considered different approaches and mindsets when it comes to attracting others, to the "chase" and building attraction, and if we're lucky, to sustaining that attraction so it turns into a fulfilling relationship. Let's turn now to something you might have overlooked in your dating quest: what you're even looking for in the first place and why.

When I was a teenager, I thought I knew exactly what I wanted in a girlfriend.

[Read this in a teenage perspective]

163

First, she had to be a ballerina because I had a couple of friends that were ballerinas, and they were pretty, fit, and fun to be around. Maybe it was a side effect of constantly being in spandex and being scrutinized, but they didn't seem to let much rattle them.

Second, they had to have a car because I drove my mother's car and had to split car time with her, which was annoying because she went shopping a lot. The year before, I was almost late to the winter dance because of my mom's dance aerobics class!

Third, they couldn't be painters, because my friend Molly was a painter and the only thing she talked about was the new art she was planning and creating. At first, it was nice to hear about something different, but it was getting old pretty fast. I intentionally sat at different table than her at lunch, so I think my message was pretty clear.

[Teenage perspective over]

To many of you, the teenage me sounds simplistic, idealistic, and shallow—call it what you will. That's certainly how I would characterize it.

The teenage me allowed random occurrences

and events to shape my views and also cared about things that had no logical connection to anything that would make a good partner. Almost everything had a shallow basis and wasn't about a person's traits or personality. Finally, there were elements that sounded great in theory but were completely unrelated to anything else in my life.

I had essentially created an ideal in my mind without considering whether it made sense for me—or whether it made sense period. That's pretty much par for the course for a teenager who hadn't even had his first kiss yet. You wouldn't expect much more depth from someone who lacks life experience and doesn't have any perspective to base his views on. You might even be impressed that a teenager could articulate three traits or features that way.

Now take that teenager's perspective and imagine it coming out of a grown adult's mouth—at thirty or even forty years old. You'd think that it would be absolutely laughable, but it doesn't sound so unnatural, does it? The truth is, we still fall prey to the same *shiny objects* approach (as in, "Ooh, look at that shiny object! I want that.") that teenagers do when we think about what we want in our partner. We are overly affected by singular experiences and attempt to extrapolate what little information we have into hard requirements or deal-breakers.

Teenage Patrick's first request was for a ballerina because they tend to be fit and pretty. *He was saying that he liked an entire group of people based on an idealized and filtered view of an occupation.*

Teenage Patrick's second request was for someone with a car. *He was saying he wanted people based on their means and resources— like looking at someone's resume or evaluating their income.*

Teenage Patrick's third request was for no painters. *He was saying that he didn't like an entire group of people because his exposure to one person had created a judgment on everyone in that group.*

We still do all of those things as adults! We say what we *want* based on what we don't really know, and we say what we *don't want* based on what we don't really know—*and* we want someone with means. We still allow the same errors in thinking to guide our decisions in what we want in a mate long after puberty.

We Are Just Guessing

More often than not, we suffer from a lack of information about the things we want and the things we don't want. We have a great time at one party but wonder why we don't enjoy other parties, not realizing that we don't know exactly *why* we had a good time—and vice versa. It's exactly the same with knowing the type of person you want to be with. Our lives aren't scientific experiments in which we can isolate and prevent confounding factors. We do the best we can with what we have, and we have to make educated assumptions and guesses along the way. We compare our experiences with so-called objective standards, with experiences from our social circle, and we come to a decision.

In the same way, people tend to think they know exactly what they want in a partner. If you ask anyone this question, you'll get a laundry list of traits that seems to come from a place of experience and knowledge. He must be tall, possess a great sense of humor, and love children. She must be adventurous and a willing traveler, drama-free, and great with your mother.

The list of traits never gets much more

specific than that, and people end up describing someone who is attractive in an idealistic way or based on incomplete information like Teenage Patrick. Taken out into the real world, shallow lists of attributes like these don't quite seem to work as well as we'd hoped, or we might find ourselves with someone who ticks all the boxes and yet who nevertheless seems all wrong for us.

I usually take this to mean that people have no idea what they actually want in a partner. A study in 2008 (Eastwick & Finkel) confirmed this fact when researchers surveyed participants in a speed-dating event. Before the event occurred, the participants completed a questionnaire about the traits they found most attractive in the opposite sex.

The questionnaire found typical results—the participants indicated they were attracted to generic and traditional traits and characteristics. Generally speaking, men placed a higher premium on physical attractiveness, while women placed higher value on status and resources.

After the speed-dating event, people were asked who they were attracted to at the event. And guess what?

There was virtually zero overlap between the traits they *said* they were looking for and the traits they were actually attracted to. People did not act according to how they answered the pre-study questionnaire—to their credit. Men showed interest in a woman's status and personality and weren't generally as shallow as they indicated previously. Women also expanded their range of what they were interested in.

In other words, people were astonishingly bad at predicting what they would be attracted to in other people. You probably didn't need a study to tell you that. The chapter on arranged marriages also provides clarity in how bad we are at predicting what matters in a relationship, and may hint at some ancient wisdom of our elders to know that we can't always be trusted to know what we want in the long term.

One reason relates to a psychological theory called the *construal-level theory* (Trope & Liberman, 2003). The theory states that psychological *distance* prompts people to think abstractly and ideally about things, while psychological *closeness* prompts people to think more concretely and realistically about things.

For example, if you don't know much about baseball, which represents psychological distance, all you can do is say that there's someone who throws the ball, someone who catches the ball, and someone who hits the ball. That's abstract thinking.

But if you played baseball in school, which represents psychological closeness, you could go on and on about baseball strategy and batting averages. That's concrete thinking.

There are a few factors that influence psychological closeness:

1. Temporal distance—time
2. Spatial distance—proximity
3. Social distance—interpersonal similarity
4. Hypothetical distance—how likely you imagine something to be

When we put the construal-level theory into the dating context, it confirms everything we knew and the prior studies found.

When people met potential romantic partners in person, there was very little psychological distance, which caused them to evaluate the person in front of them in an entirely different way than if they merely thought about the type of romantic partner they wanted—the psychological distance of which would cause them to describe ideal platitudes and traits.

In other words, our daydreams when we're by ourselves are nothing close to how we evaluate people that are right in front of us. That's one reason people don't know what they want in a partner. We are actually in our heads too much, away from the people we seek to meet, and this causes us to ruminate in psychological distance. The more we plan and make a vision board full of traits we want, the more detached from our actual preferences we are.

Another reason is that people tend to be self-centered and focused on themselves. When we think about our mate preferences, we're often not thinking about attraction and what we actually like. We're thinking about our self-interests and how we would benefit from that type of partner. Everything else flows from that self-interest. Self-interest and benefit can easily become conflated with attraction and even love.

For example, you want a partner with high earning potential because it will bode well for you in the future. You're not thinking about attraction—you're thinking about a long-term view and how your mate will help you reach the vision you have for your own life. It's all very logical and rational—you might even call it cold and calculating.

Of course, logic and rationality rarely mix with the real world of dating and relationships.

Finally, we regularly formulate theories about what we find attractive in others because we think we should feel certain ways and want certain things. It's what we've been socialized with since birth and continue to be socialized with through our parents, families, friends, and the media at large. We are told what to think without considering whether it's the best course of action (type of partner) for us.

If you've been raised since birth to only love pine trees while simultaneously being told that oak trees are bad for you, there's not much chance you'll deviate from pine trees, even if they make you sneeze. Oak trees might be your exact fit, but you'll be fighting years of indoctrination to even be open to them. Even if you're unhappy with pine trees, that doesn't tell you that oak trees will fit you either!

This isn't as bleak as it sounds. But it's worth remembering to keep your focus where it matters—not on fixed superficial interests or assumptions ("I want a girl who likes rock") but on how a dynamic relationship would *function*. Without culture, family expectation, or lazy stereotypes, what do we want from another person and what can we offer them? The better we can answer this question, the better our chances of actually finding the relationship that is good for us—and not just what we think is good for us!

Universal Desires

And yet (another disclaimer, of course), there are scientifically proven triggers for attraction and arousal. While we might not understand what we are looking for from a personality standpoint, there are universal traits that we want from a psychological and biological standpoint.

Excitement. This springs from one of the most interesting theories of arousal—the *misattribution of arousal* theory.

The misattribution of arousal is the proposition that people aren't necessarily aroused by what's in front of them. Instead, for one reason or another, they enter a state of physical arousal first, and then they attribute the cause of that arousal to what is currently in front of them. They make an assumption that because they are physically aroused in the presence of their partner, for example, that their partner was the one arousing them.

Why is this called the *misattribution* of arousal theory? It's because we aren't always correct about what turns us on and gets us physically aroused. This is something you can take advantage of.

In 1974, Donald Dutton and Arthur Aron tested this theory by having two groups of men interact with an attractive female immediately after crossing a bridge. In one group, the bridge was relatively unstable and scary, and the other group's bridge was stable and secure. The attractive female gave her phone number to each and every participant. What ended up happening?

The men in the first group, the scary bridge group, were twice as likely to call the attractive female and ask her on a date after the study was over.

What accounted for this massive difference? Males in the scary bridge group were already aroused when they met and spoke with the attractive female. As a result, they contacted the female because they misattributed their arousal to the female, not the scary bridge they had just crossed. In other words, they believed they were feeling sexual arousal from the female instead of plain old physiological arousal from the fear of the bridge.

The more physically anxious, excited, and even fearful you are, no matter the cause, the more attractive and arousing you will find the people near you because of the misattribution of arousal theory. Here, the scary bridge physically aroused the men in that group and pumped up their adrenaline and bodily functions in a way similar to when we are sexually aroused.

This certainly happens more than you might think. People misattribute physiological arousal to sexual attraction all the time. Many even do it by instinct.

For example, have you ever taken a date—or been taken—on a roller coaster, flying, or something else that's thrilling over a dinner date? Even a scary movie qualifies here. If you have, or if you've heard this advice parroted around, it's because it takes advantage of the misattribution of arousal theory. Your date gets physiologically aroused and excited by the roller coaster or scary movie, grabs your hand out of fear, and then attributes the butterflies in his or her stomach to you and not the triple-faced ghost on the movie screen.

It's also what dating reality shows like *The Bachelor* and *The Bachelorette* use in spades. They'll send their contestants out on thrilling and dangerous dates like skydiving or deep ocean shark fighting. How can you expect sparks not to fly after that due to this theory? Creating excitement is a no-brainer if you want to instantly create attraction.

Gender-specific triggers. Though arousal is universal in some ways, it can also be incredibly nuanced. There is a very marked gender difference in the basics of arousal— the hows and whys, even.

HENCE MEN DO THE AIIROACH

Researcher and author Emily Nagoski discovered through various studies that men are spontaneously aroused, while women become aroused in response to something.

MEN
MUST
ESCALATE It means that men spontaneously have the desire to have sex, and women have that same desire only in response to that man.

176

This is the cause of what many couples consider mismatched libidos—the man will be the only one to initiate sex, while the woman may be happy to have it but will never outwardly show signs of desire and lust.

YOU ESCALATE / THEN SHE RESPONDS IF SHE WANTS TO

This commonly causes men to feel unwanted and neglected, but it's a matter of adjusting expectations because women don't function in the same spontaneous manner. In fact, Nagoski estimated that up to one-third of women have primarily responsive sexual arousal, whereas the vast majority of men have primarily spontaneous sexual arousal.

How can we bridge the gap here? It's the knowledge that women need to be aroused first before they want to have sex, while men continually just want sex. Their desire may not actually be different; you just have to set the conditions for one gender a little bit more.

KEY NAV POINT - LEAD

The lesson for men is that you have to seduce women first, and then they will be open to sex. Women are looking for cues from you to be aroused because it won't happen for them out of thin air. The lesson for women is to not feel guilty or shame if you have been told you have a low sex drive or libido. You just may have responsive sexual arousal, and your

177

partner needs to break the ice a little bit more first—or you can break it yourself first, but don't have the expectation that you should spontaneously feel horny or aroused while shopping for apples.

Recent studies published in the sexology journal of *Archives of Sexual Behavior* confirm the assertion that women need to be outwardly desired more than men before they feel aroused themselves.

THE
APPROACH
STYLE
&
CUTE

The studies found that a major part of female sexual arousal and fantasies was perceiving themselves to be desirable, irresistible, and like men couldn't control themselves around them. If a woman perceives herself to be the object of desire, lust, and affection, then her sexual arousal and appetite are generally higher than if not.

FIRST
STEP -
STRONG
APPROACH
WITH
SMILE
TEASE

That certainly adds fuel to the fire that women are more responsive and dependent on signals from their partner in order to feel attractive and sexually aroused. I hope the men reading are paying attention here. Women won't typically be the ones to spontaneously come up behind you and start copping a feel, but they won't mind if you do (if you have previous signs of consent and attraction).

And if you do it consistently and in a way that makes them feel like you can't help or control yourself around them, you'll be able to have sex more consistently because you are catering to their responsive sense of sexual arousal.

Laughter. A sense of humor is highly attractive to the opposite sex. However, again, there was a big difference between how genders perceived this seemingly simple statement. The female definition of a good sense of humor was when the male made them laugh, but the male definition of a good sense of humor was when the female laughed at their jokes. Another researcher analyzed over three thousand dating profiles, and the data lined up with the previous findings: women tended to describe their ability to appreciate humor, whereas men tended to describe their ability to produce humor.

It also lines up with traditional gender roles of the suitor and the recipient, so perhaps no matter how close we get to true gender equality, there are still hardwired preferences when it comes to romantic and sexual relations.

Voice. Dr. Susan Hughes of Albright College

discovered that these hardwired preferences that prefer biological differences are highly present in the voices of the opposite sex. Women were found to be more attracted to men who spoke in lower, baritone or bass voices, and men were found to be far more attracted to women who spoke in higher, soprano pitches. If you want a reference for how that sounds, just think Marilyn Monroe singing *Happy Birthday* to John F. Kennedy or any of Barry White's songs and you have the general idea.

What we've learned about desirable traits is that even though we are consistently wrong about what we want, at least there are biological bases we can rely on. At least it makes us a little more predictable in our lack of accuracy.

Selflessness is Sexy

There is one final trait that is so universally attractive that I wanted to spend a bit more time on it. Whether you call it altruism, kindness, or selflessness, people like people who are caring and helpful to others. In fact, evolutionary psychologists believe that this human behavior is not just great for the maintenance of a healthy and cooperative society, but it also has direct benefits for the individual being kind.

In 2013, researchers at the University of Bristol found that both men and women were attracted to what they called "helping behaviors." When study participants were asked to rate people on attractiveness, those they explicitly described as being kind and helpful were deemed as more attractive. It's worth noting, however, that they were being assessed as potential *long-term sexual partners*; as for short-term flings and one-night stands, the finding was that women still found kindness more attractive, but that kindness didn't seem to matter much for men.

These findings shouldn't surprise us much: nobody truly wants to interact with someone who is selfish, mean, or inconsiderate. There are social but also biological reasons that human beings have evolved to care for one another, and to signal their value to others by being considerate, helpful, and conscientious.

Even if you've never given it much thought, chances are you want someone in your life who is kind and thoughtful. Do people sometimes choose to be with those who are mean and unkind? Yes. But they tend to love people like this *in spite of* their meanness, not because of it. While those who have low self-esteem may settle for poor treatment, it's a pretty standard human trait to want to be around those who are respectful, kind, attentive, and know how to listen—male or female.

When you are selfless, you are communicating a few very attractive qualities to potential mates. You are telling them that you are secure enough in your own identity and feeling of self-worth that you don't need to constantly focus on yourself in any interaction. This signals a relaxed, confident person.

When you are selfless, you broadcast that generosity of spirit that makes you seem positive and well balanced. People are attracted to those who are not always trying to stroke their own ego or get something out of others, but instead are so comfortable and content in themselves that they have extra to give to others. This is a really empowered position to take!

Finally, if you're selfless, you come across as more easy-going, more open, and more intelligent. You may even seem like a better lover—who doesn't want to be with someone selfless in bed?

Of course, selfless doesn't mean you're a long-suffering martyr or that you use kindness in a passive aggressive way. You have to be *genuinely* kind, i.e., not pretend to be nice because you're expecting a reward for it. It's less attractive if someone is being helpful or kind simply out of begrudging sense of duty and obligation. Rather, people are attracted to those who have a strong moral compass, and sincerely enjoy doing the good in the world and acting toward the things they care about. You may not hear it often, but people with values and principles demonstrate to others that they have self-respect and a mission/purpose in life—and that's very sexy.

This is useful information both as we try to attract the people we desire and when we try to make ourselves more attractive to them. Forget the idea that nice guys finish last. Genuine kindness, concern for others, and thoughtfulness are always appealing in a mate, male or female. Look for people who are authentically caring and cooperative and commit to being that kind of person yourself.

A little playing hard to get, a little uncertainty, a little frisson and tension—none of that means you forget your manners or treat others with anything other than respect and thoughtfulness.

The media likes to perpetuate the story that girls like bad boys, and that men go weak in the knees for bitchy girls. But it's just not true. While meanness, cruelty, or disinterest may capture some people's attention initially, it's the kind of attraction that won't be sustained long term. Creating a successful long-term sexual relationship requires both parties to be kind, sweet, and caring to one another.

Sounds kind of obvious, doesn't it?

Happiness is Sexy—If You're a Woman

Quick, which kind of man do women like most, the happy smiling dude or the dark brooding guy who's always scowling a little?

Though selflessness, kindness, and compassion are universally attractive, research published in 2011 by Tracey and Beall in the journal *Emotion* found that the appeal of "bad boys" is actually down to women finding happy men less sexually attractive than sullen ones. The researchers found a dramatic sex difference here—men found happy, smiling woman more attractive than sulky ones, but the opposite was true for what women were sexually attracted to.

The display and expression of emotion and how it affects attractiveness has not been extensively studied, but the common belief that a smile is attractive may not be entirely true. A smile may indeed make people think you are friendly, trustworthy, and kind, but it may not make you seem more *sexually* attractive—at least to women.

The researchers asked one thousand adults to rate the attractiveness of pictures of people who were demonstrating happiness (smiling), pride (chin up, standing tall), and shame (lowered gaze). The women liked best the men who demonstrated pride and, surprisingly, shame, but were less impressed with those who were simply happy. Men instead rated the smiling happy women as most attractive, finding proud women least attractive.

So, if you're a guy trying to make a good first impression, should you pout and mope? The study's co-author Alec Beall says, "It is important to remember that this study explored first-impressions of sexual attraction to images of the opposite sex. We were not asking participants if they thought these targets would make a good boyfriend or wife—we wanted their gut reactions on carnal, sexual attraction." So, while being dark and mysterious may be great for initially catching attention and sparking attraction, most studies find that in the long run, people overwhelmingly prefer nice personalities and those who express positive emotions.

If we look more closely at the postures and expressions rated as most attractive for men, they make sense: women may prefer men who appear self-assured, competent, and confident. This implies a certain degree of power and competence, which are broadly considered attractive for men in most cultures. Smiling, however, is sometimes suggested by evolutionary psychologists to signal a lack of dominance.

Again, there is nothing especially "feminine" about the emotion of happiness or its expression; rather, these studies seem to show that at least in the earliest moments of raw physical sexual attraction, we are still guided by our most primitive and basic impulses.

So many of our (frankly sexist and outdated) rules for dating and relationship norms rest on gender assumptions that studies like this appear to confirm. However, what about the fact that men who displayed shame (such as looking down or acting bashful) were also rated as very attractive? Both men and women found this emotion attractive, perhaps because it conveyed an attractive awareness of social norms, which may in turn communicate intelligence and cooperativeness.

How can we apply this to our dating lives right now? That's simple: if you're a woman, a smile really is your most attractive asset. Openly express happiness, joy, delight, and contentment, and you will automatically seem more appealing than a woman who is displeased in some way. If you're a man, realize that the main thing you want to convey in the very earliest first impression is that you are competent, powerful, and in charge of yourself. You don't need to come across as *unhappy*. Rather, you want to give the impression of being in command of yourself, confident, in control, and competent. A little serious.

Depending on your personality, you might like to come across as a serious and intense intellectual, or you might decide your style is more rebellious, moody, and dark. Whatever fits for you, though, remember the other finding of the study: that the expression of "shame" was also deemed very attractive. So don't be cocky or boastful; instead, try to come across as quietly confident in what you know you're awesome at, yet willing to be humble and deferential with those things you aren't.

Beyond first impressions, it's probably best to switch your tactic—for longer-term dating and relationships, emotional intelligence, and honest expression are more attractive for both sexes. Dark and mysterious may work like a charm late at night in a club, but once you've dated someone for a few weeks or months, it's attractive for both sexes to be emotionally forthcoming. Initial attraction is often based on our more primal, instinctual, and biological drives, whereas mature and healthy long-term relationships develop after that, steered by our rational conscious mind. So, though a woman might find a "bad boy" kind of hot on a superficial, purely physical level, she probably wants a little more emotional maturity by the second date!

Takeaways:

- We often think we know what we want

based on singular experiences, stereotypes, or simple social pressures. But we are typically very, very wrong.

- In fact, most of the time, we are just making educated guesses. Psychological distance is deceptive, and we often confuse what we want with what benefits us from a self-interest standpoint. In reality, what we do know is simply what we don't want. This is not the same as wanting the opposite of what we don't want.

- Despite our own internal confusions, there are certain scientifically proven traits we do seek in mates that are more related to biological imperatives. We are subconsciously drawn to excitement and arousal, fulfilling gender-specific arousal triggers, a sense of humor, and masculine and feminine voices.

- Research shows that while smiling and expressing happiness can make people like and trust you, when it comes to relationships and dating, this is not always the case: men find smiling, happy women most sexually attractive, but women tend to rate as more attractive those men who express pride (i.e., competence and self-assuredness) and shame (lowered gaze and awareness of social norms). At least initially, expressing happiness is theorized to convey a lack of status or dominance.

Chapter 7. Acts of the Amorous Nature

Much of this book has been focused on how to get to this point: intimate relations.

When you have successfully engineered attraction to the point where you can consummate that attraction, congratulations! You've reached the peak and there is nothing left to think about. You've won and everything is downhill from here, right?

That would be nice if that were the truth. It seems like the end goal might be to have sex with someone, but in reality, the goal is to have sustained, intimate sex with someone. That is a very different goal because of how much it encompasses and the hoops to jump through for it.

In essence, we're talking about how to achieve remarkable sex. Some people might view sex like pizza; even bad pizza is still a good meal. But if we want to fulfill our real goals of sex that accentuates an emotional bond and that can lead to a relationship, we can't just take our cues from pornography. Sex is one of the most primal drives—as such, as with before, this can make us relatively predictable in a way that you can take advantage of.

Here's the thing about great, toe-curling sex: it isn't what we think it is. We have continually been told it's one spicy "secret" sex position or delving into blindfolds and whips and chains just because it's novel and exciting. At least, that's what magazine covers have sold us.

Much of what we think makes for great sex is split into one of two camps. It's either about specific techniques you can be doing better or more of, or it's about spicing up your sex life in ways that simply blow your mind because they tap into your deeper and darker fetishes.

While those are true and undoubtedly help, they are also misleading. They can sometimes cause us to skip over the basics and what really matters, like buying a car with a terrible engine but a nice paint job and door handles. You might think you're going to have a smooth ride, and you might for the first couple of times, but it's not destined for success and can undermine your other efforts at creating remarkable sex from the inside and out.

Finally, it is a total myth that attraction or even love is enough to guarantee great sex. Think of it this way: all babies are born with the ability to learn how to speak and to use language, and eventually, most of us do. But that doesn't mean we don't have to be taught how to speak, how to write, how to read, and how to converse properly with other people. Thus, language is both an innate primal drive yet also something we need to learn to develop and master. Sex is similar. We all have the inbuilt emotional and physiological machinery to crave and seek out sex, but it's another thing entirely to have that kind of "conversation" with someone else. While raw attraction and affection are necessary, they are not sufficient conditions for truly satisfying sex.

Elements

If wonderful sex isn't about novelty, isn't about exciting fetishes, and isn't about the specific techniques and positions, what is it about? Well, this might be a relief for you if you feel that sex just doesn't need to involve superhuman fitness or leather props. For those people who are inexperienced with relationships, the prospect of engaging sexually with someone can seem hugely intimidating. It's easier to imagine there's a quick set of rules or tricks that you can rely on to help you choreograph the encounter. But are there really?

Researcher Peggy Kleinplatz conducted multiple studies on the issue and found one particular set of elements that were far more indicative to great sex than novelty or spiciness. In fact, those elements that you'll always read about on the covers of magazines did not figure into the results. They didn't report helping people's sex lives at all! In the end, it was advice that sounded good in theory but didn't make a difference in practice.

No toys or tongue tricks are needed to create remarkable sex. Kleinplatz also found in the study that actual orgasms and attraction were not part of what made remarkable sex. This is good news for some and terrible news for others. It almost sounds like I am about to sell you the one special technique that blows all others out of the water, but it's really about bringing it back to the basics.

She found eight elements that thousands of respondents in her studies listed as the most important, and these elements were consistent across all age groups, genders, ethnicities, and even locations. The eight elements of great sex are listed below, and we'll go through each in greater detail.

The elements are:

1. Presence
2. Connection
3. Intimacy
4. Communication
5. Authenticity
6. Bliss
7. Exploration
8. Vulnerability

As you might figure, some of these elements are fulfilled by what magazines tell us to do— with novelty, whips, and chains. However, you might miss the point if you don't think about the actual purpose and intention behind the elements. If you dive in with the props and loaded expectations and you *don't* have any of the above elements, you're more likely to have disappointing sex rather than the romp promised by that glossy magazine.

Presence. What does presence mean? It's not a magnetic presence at a party; rather, it's the act of being *present* and in the moment. This is when you're not preoccupied and you're completely focused on the person in front of you and the act that is occurring. You have only one thing in your mind, and that is the other person and how they feel.

You act like the other person is your world for the moment—and they are, aren't they? You have to commit all the way with your time and attention and fully immerse yourself in the moment.

You can't be a spectator, judge, critic, or passive participant. You're not thinking about your emails, your television shows, or what you want to have for dinner. If you're on this wavelength, then it's no wonder your sex life is on thin ice.

You are simply there, fully present, with nothing else on your mind. The world comprises only two individuals, one bed, and passion. Everything else is put on the back burner and essentially disappears. That's

196

what it means to be present.

It's easy to see how we can fall prey to not being present. We all have numerous responsibilities throughout the day. But various studies peg the average length of sexual intercourse at anywhere from seven to sixteen minutes. It should not be a tremendous struggle to shut down your brain for that amount of time and simply lose yourself. Just imagine how present you would be having sex in a cabin in the woods with no television or internet access. That's the kind of focus and connection you want every time.

They deserve it, and so do you. How would you feel if someone prefaced sex with, "Let's be quick. I have more work," or if they continually looked at a clock during the act? Being present during sex, you will be more attentive, respond better to people's signs, and care more about their satisfaction.

Connection. This is when you feel like you're in sync with the other person mentally and emotionally. You understand things without having to say them, you know each other, and you feel an emotional pull toward them. You have electric chemistry and both of you know it.

Contrast that to a one-night stand, where you probably have very little emotional investment. The act and ensuing pleasure is minimized because there's little at stake and it's purely physical. With emotional connection, you create something with intimacy, and you are fusing your bodies and minds together for a brief moment in time.

Connection is feeling a spark with the other person holistically, not just physically. You like them on more than just a physical level, and you can experience feeling bonded with them. When you have a strong connection, you might say things like, "Our bodies just moved together and we didn't have to say a word."

Intimacy. This can be distinguished from connection because intimacy is about a deeper caring and love for the other person, whereas connection might be momentary and fleeting. When you have that type of feeling toward someone, then sex becomes more than just a physical act. It becomes an act of love and sharing.

This is also a complete acceptance of the other person and their flaws, and it involves you opening yourself to them. This happens when you respect and care for someone, and it is a byproduct of a healthy relationship. There is trust, vulnerability, and the feeling that you can bare yourself to someone else.

Communication. Communication is key in friendships and relationships, so it should be in sex as well. From another angle, sex is an activity with a partner (or multiple partners), so it only makes sense that there should be a healthy amount of communication to coordinate, discuss, direct, and request whenever appropriate. Greater satisfaction simply occurs when collaboration is possible, and collaboration is possible with better communication.

Along with communication comes a heightened attention and empathy to your partner's needs and desires. This is important because sex should not be approached like a self-centered act—it's an act with one goal: an orgasm for both parties. In fact, the best sex focuses on the other person's pleasure, so communicating what those might be is paramount.

Communication should be open, there should be mutual support, and there should be an ability for both parties to express exactly what they want or dislike without the fear of judgment or rejection. This is where talking about fetishes and kinks comes in, because open and honest communication should allow those without feeling self-conscious or judged.

You should ideally be able to communicate about everything, from exactly what you hate to the tiny things you love. The point is to keep a running dialogue going because preferences can always change, and you need to be able to adapt to them.

Authenticity. Remarkable sex is honest and open. It's authentic because you aren't hiding anything. Not only are you making yourself completely open to the other person, but you're trusting your body with them. If you can let go and make yourself vulnerable, it can be powerful.

You are being authentic and honest about what you like and dislike, and you are encouraging the same in the other person. You are having sex for pleasure, love, or expression, not for any nefarious reason or ulterior motives. Put another way, you feel that you can be genuine in your expression, that you aren't hiding or inhibiting your desires, and that you can be completely transparent and honest with the other person.

You should feel free to do, touch, lick, and suck what you like without embarrassment or feelings of judgment. This works both ways, because both parties need to ensure that they don't make the other feel judged or guilty. Truly authentic sex is liberating because you feel like you can do what you like without having to restrain yourself. Of course, that works best with communication and the other elements in this chapter.

Bliss. This is a loaded word. What does it mean here?

It means that amazing sex is more than just an act. It's a mental state of mind, and it creates something that is more than the sum of its parts. It creates an emotion of transcendence and bliss: a peaceful state of mind characterized by happiness, transformation, introspection, and fulfillment.

It's a state of nirvana. You're in a world that consists of only two people, and you feel like there's nowhere else you'd rather be at that moment. You are exchanging mental, emotional, and physical energy. You are basking in their glow and pleasure.

Bliss just means you feel fulfilled and satisfied

after the act, with no regret. Your head is clear, you feel more at peace with the world, and you have gained perspective on life. Some people might have sex to calm their nerves, out of boredom, out of hatred, or out of pure lust. Blissfully remarkable sex is when sex occurs as an expression of love and fulfillment with the other person.

You can even think about bliss in religious terms. You feel a sense of peace that you may receive after praying or a particularly powerful religious service. That's what sex can do at times. It can feel like a holy experience.

Exploration. This, of course, is also where kink and spicy sex come into play.

Sex can sometimes get boring, even with all of the other elements in this chapter, so exploration, or at least being willing to explore and indulge, is a key to remarkable sex.

It's fun. It breaks you out of your routine, and it makes sex novel and interesting, which is necessary sometimes. It allows you to discover what you really want and to test uncharted waters. When you can explore your sexuality, you can also discover what makes you orgasm the longest and hardest. It might not be what you think, and you never would have discovered it if you didn't open your mind.

Exploration can sometimes mean a certain amount of risk, but risk in this context isn't really risk. It's just stepping outside of your comfort zone, and there aren't any negative consequences other than to say, "Well, I didn't like that as much as I thought I would. Next!" The only risk here is that you might buy something expensive to explore a fetish and end up hating it and feel that you wasted that money.

Exploration puts the fun back into sex. It makes it an unpredictable ride that is the essence of playing. You can follow your instincts and discover new kinks you like, or you can just allow curiosity to guide you. You can play sex games to have fun during long car rides, or you can try to make the other person orgasm as many times as possible within twenty-four hours.

These are all possible with exploration and stepping outside of your comfort zone. Remarkable sex is comfortable with laughter, getting messy, and new acts for their own sake. It doesn't restrain or judge them—it encourages them.

Vulnerability. Scary. We all know what happens when we make ourselves vulnerable. It allows us to be hurt.

However, remarkable sex requires this because of the positives and benefits it can allow. It allows us to fully embrace someone and let them into our hearts and psyches and bodies. We are physically naked during sex, but vulnerability allows us to drop our mental and emotional shields. You are trusting someone and surrendering to them. This is scary.

You are shedding your defense mechanisms, your anxieties, and your egos to the sexual encounter. You are stripping bare, putting yourself on a shelf for judgment, and trusting that the other person will celebrate you rather than reject you. You are devoted to them and trust that they are devoted to you. You say and do things that you would never do to other people, but here you aren't embarrassed because it's what is in your heart.

In fact, you say exactly what you want to say and do that as well. That's vulnerability—

when you don't filter and you allow people inside your walls. Fantastic and remarkable sex is pulling others closer to you when you feel the exact opposite impulse and you want to keep someone at arm's length.

Again, you can see that none of these elements of remarkable sex are what we usually think they are: novelty and techniques. Those are included and a part of some of these elements, but not the underlying aspect that makes it so satisfying and pleasurable.

Kleinplatz's findings are important because they tell us that wonderful sex does not depend on flexibility, athleticism, or being choked so hard that you nearly fall unconscious. Wonderful sex is for everyone because it happens when you simply focus on the other person, give yourself freely, and have an authentic connection.

While that may be harder to find than a one-night stand, it also means that everyone in a relationship can indeed have remarkable sex. Nothing keeps you from it except yourself. If you find yourself unable to satisfy any of the elements, the problem is never in the sex itself. Nearly everyone has the mental and physical capability to fulfill Kleinplatz's factors for great sex. It may not be easy, however, and thus it comes down to how much you care and want the sex to improve. You have the blueprint; what you do with it is up to you.

It's never a bad thing to do a bit more exploring, however.

What Actually Turns Women On

In the beginning of this book, we spoke about how those first crucial moments of attraction have powerful roots in our primal, evolutionary history. In the beginning, lust, chemistry, and outright attraction play a big role in who we choose to connect with—and knowing how to leverage that information can make us more appealing and magnetic to others.

However, after a relationship is underway, a completely new set of skills comes into play—the spark has been lit, but the fire needs to be maintained.

Connection, communication, vulnerability . . . how many men might roll their eyes at this list and wonder what it has to do with sex? Men who are unsuccessful with women may know in vivid detail what turns *them* on and simply assume that the woman of their dreams will be one who happily goes along with that, end of story. They make terrible lovers because, on a most fundamental level, they lack imagination and empathy—without imagination, they cannot see the world or the sex act through anyone's perspective but their own, and without empathy, they don't care enough to do anything about those differences.

Interested in knowing what turns a woman on? If there's a woman in your life, that's simple: ask her.

A study in the Journal of *Sex and Marital Therapy*, however, has a few key points you might like to consider. After surveying almost seven hundred women about what made them desire their sexual partners more, they found three recurring themes (you'll notice that none of them refer to a male's anatomy, his physical appearance, technique in the sack, or bank balance!):

Intimacy

No surprise here! Plenty of closeness, affection, understanding, affirmation, and caring were considered by many women to be *prerequisites* to sex. This is important. While men may see sex as a way to arrive at more closeness, for women it's the other way around: sex is an expression of closeness. So, a man may seek out sex because he wants to feel good and close to his partner, but a women will seek out sex only after she feels good and close to her partner . . . and then sex is almost a celebration or expression of that fact.

Celebrated Otherness

If you're straight, a big part of your attraction comes from the tension in the difference between men and women, i.e., the "otherness" between them. A feeling of separateness, of mysterious and unknowable difference, can spur attraction. The differences are celebrated—even though you can get really, really close, there is always still a part of you that is autonomous and unknown. In that space where things are not resolved lies some potential, and that's sexy. What does this mean for the man who wants to make a woman happy?

It means you acknowledge that she's a woman, that she's different from you, and that you love it and want to celebrate it and enjoy it with her rather than try to dissect or

208

control or dominate it. The irony is that if you can acknowledge that you will never completely own or possess her, then you actually allow for more intimacy and passion.

Object of Desire Affirmation

This one is tricky for women to express to men, because they have historically been so bad at understanding what it means. Women never want to be objectified. But they want to feel that they are desired by the people that they desire. They want to feel loved and praised for who they are, and are turned on when they know that they are someone else's turn on!

This one is easy to put into practice: make the woman you're with feel like a million bucks. Tell her what you love about her body. Tell her you've been fantasizing about her. Compliment her clothing or jewelry. Let her know you think she's one hot tamale and you don't care how many times she hears it!

Be careful, though—women want to be seen as beautiful sex-goddesses by the men they love, and they want to know, frankly, that they're hot. But that's not *all* they want to be seen as. Never imply that the only value she has in your eyes is as a sex object.

So, really, the age-old question of "what women want" is not really that mysterious after all. Women want the sense of trust and safety that comes with being emotionally intimate with someone, and this allows them to open up sexually. Men may misunderstand this, because it's not how they themselves think. A man may consider emotional intimacy a poor substitute for sex, or something that only builds after sex, or simply something irrelevant that gets in the way.

For those who are only concerned with one-night stands, and those who don't especially care if their partners are satisfied, any number of pick-up tricks and techniques can get a few extra notches on the bed post. These people may love sex, but they don't necessarily love or even understand women. For those who want deeper, more fulfilling, and more sustainable relationships that include plenty of good sex, they need to understand that for women, sex and emotions are wrapped up closely together.

Make a woman feel safe, understood, and respected, and sex will never be an issue. Make her feel valued for the unique person she is. Play with mystery and discovery. Be

210

genuinely interested in what makes her happy and what her needs are, rather than approaching the relationship primarily with your own needs at the forefront. Oh, and it doesn't hurt to tell her often that she's hot stuff.

Getting Kinky

Fifty Shades of Grey. There, I mentioned it.

The infamous book was important for introducing the concept of kinky and abnormal sexual practices into the general population who might never have given it a second thought. It shone a flashlight into the dark depths of the kink world and gave it a name—Christian Grey. It gave people an outlet to explore and provided some kind of framework into things they vaguely enjoyed but had no way of articulating.

Kinky sex has always been a point of captivation for people because it involves sex, a topic usually greeted with blushes, giggles, and knowing glances. Fascination ensues when people realize they could be having much more fulfilling, more adventurous sex than they are currently having.

Kink arrived loudly and is here to stay, but it is not without its critics. The critics are largely a factor of judgments and a misunderstanding of the simple fact that people have different tastes.

It's such a simple analogy that I've used it time and time again; some people love football and some people love baseball. If you ask them to articulate the reason for their preference, most people will say, "I don't know, just because I do." Now substitute any number of fetishes for football and vanilla sex with baseball. What's the real difference here? Would you prevent someone from watching football just as you would purport to prevent empowering someone to seize their own pleasure? Would you say that baseball is boring and that the only way to enjoy sports is to go for the real stuff (i.e., football)?

But the science of kink and how it relates to attraction is fascinating and indicates that it might go deeper than a simple preference for football or leather whips.

It turns out that some of us might actually be biologically predisposed to some sexual kinks and couldn't help it if we tried. Neural mapping, the literal physical configuration of our brains, might explain our proclivity for some sexual kinks. If not the brain structure, then the neurotransmitters might explain it. At least, those are two of the theories I will explore shortly.

What is the science of kink and the cause behind some of our deepest and darkest desires? There are five distinct theories that have been set forth that attempt to explain why we like what we do (Justin Lehmiller, Harvard University).

Adjacent brain theory. This is a theory put forth by Dr. V.S. Ramachandran of the University of California, San Diego, and utilizes an understanding of the brain's physical structure to explain kinky interests.

Different parts of the brain govern different body parts and bodily functions. This has been proven extensively, to the point where we now understand exactly where in the brain speech, personality, and anger occur. There are also specific parts of the brain that govern sexual impulses.

Now, it's not as if there are walls in the brain to keep these parts from interacting, talking, and physically overlapping with each other. The adjacent brain theory states that adjacent regions of the brain do in fact show associated activity, which means that the brain region that controls sexual impulse may very well be adjacent to the brain region that controls anger or specific body parts.

For example, the adjacent brain theory easily explains the common foot fetish because the brain regions responsible for sexual impulses, the genitalia, and the feet are close to each other and interact. When there is brain activity in one region, there is some brain activity in all adjacent regions.

The adjacent brain theory explains many aspects of kink, specifically ones that involve sexual infatuations with nonsexual body parts. But that is only a sliver of the range of kinks that exist, and the following theories can address most of them.

Pavlovian conditioning theory. Even if you don't have any interest in psychology, you are probably familiar with Ivan Pavlov and his dog.

Pavlov conducted experiments on his dog to test the subconscious routines that are created in response to predictable stimuli. He began serving dinner to his dog and accompanied dinner with ringing a bell. The dog salivated in anticipation of the food. Soon, Pavlov removed the dinner entirely and only rang the bell. The dog still salivated as if the food were present.

It showed that when people were conditioned to respond to two stimuli, the same response will come with only one stimulus present.

In the 1960s, a group of men were shown images of naked women interspersed with images of boots. As predictable by conditioning, the men were conditioned to respond with sexual arousal to the two stimuli, and when they were shown only pictures of the boots, they still responded by being sexually aroused.

This study proved that it's possible to form sexual associations with just about anything if the requisite amount of conditioning (voluntary or not) has occurred.

If you have sex or are aroused in the presence of a green teddy bear, all subsequent teddy bears or green furry objects might be enough to trigger your libido. Some might call that a kink, while some might call that a normal Saturday night. The key to this theory is that there is repeated exposure during periods of sexual arousal—it can even be certain smells, locations, or articles of clothing.

Gross-out theory. The gross-out theory was put forth by Lehmiller, and it essentially states that when people are sexually aroused, they care much less about anything else, including things that would detract from their sense of arousal. Notably, their *disgust impulse* is reduced.

In other words, when you are highly sexually aroused, you just want to get off or have an orgasm, and nothing besides pending bodily harm will throw you off that goal. Sounds about right to me. Sometimes you might inadvertently play with or stumble into things that would normally disgust you, such as feces, bodily fluids, or anal play. But then you realize that you didn't mind it, or even liked it, so you continue to integrate it into your sex life.

I recall a story from a friend I won't name who had recently broken his leg that epitomizes exactly how the gross-out theory works in real life. He was also newly single and had a hot date that he had to struggle to get to in his crutches. The date went well, and matters got hot and heavy back at her apartment later that night. I received a call at 7:00 a.m. the next morning from my friend begging me to come pick him up because he thought he had broken his leg again during vigorous sex.

Clearly, the gross-out theory applies in a wider sense as well.

Pain theory. *It hurts so good.*

Decades of research in neuroscience have shown that neurotransmitters, the chemicals in our brain that help us process our external world, are used for multiple purposes. There are only so many neurotransmitters, and they are released in certain combinations and batches to influence how good or bad we feel.

It just so happens that most of the neurotransmitters involved in sexual pleasure and pain are the same, such as serotonin, dopamine, and adrenaline.

It's as if the external signals are processed and sent to the brain on the same highway. So if pain and sexual pleasure both independently release similar combinations of neurotransmitters in our brains, then it makes too much sense to just combine the two.

This would explain the origin of many aspects of kink, such as physical dominance, whips, chains, choking, spanking, and even autoerotic asphyxiation. People don't realize they are doing it not just for the direct physical pleasure, but also the release of sweet dopamine and serotonin in their brains.

One might suppose that the ever-popular rape fantasy also slots into this category. Rape play similarly releases adrenaline, dopamine, and serotonin. This means that the pain in the *pain theory* doesn't have to be actual physical pain. As long as there is the element of threat and anticipation of pain, it's enough of a threat for the proper neurotransmitters to be released and work toward sexual arousal.

The pain theory and the gross-out theory explain many of the kinks that are beyond the realm of many people's understanding.

Subjective normal theory. The last theory to explain the appeal of kink and kinky sex derives from a study conducted by Meredith Chivers in 2014.

She gathered an all-female group of subjects and split them based on whether they were interested in BDSM (whips, chains, leather, and such) or not. Both groups watched two types of pornography: kinky and vanilla.

The women that were interested in BDSM had the same rate of vaginal blood flow as the non-kinky women who watched vanilla pornography. Likewise, when the kinky women watched vanilla porn, their blood flow did not increase at all. This was a predictable result in some ways. People were aroused by what they indicated their preference was, but people were not aroused by what they were not interested in.

People just have different desires and concepts of what an arousing sexual encounter looks like, and they aren't interested in other people's concepts. This study suggests that there is nothing neurologically abnormal about people that have kinkier sexual desires than others.

Some people enjoy sour foods and some people love salty foods. In theory, we are biologically the same, but we all have slight variations, and these variations don't mean our tongues are defective. Everyone has their subjective version of what's normal and vanilla, even though it might be shocking and extreme to someone else.

So the fifth and final theory of what causes kink? It completely reframes what kink is— it's just a preference, not an indication of anything suspicious or unbalanced. Nothing out of the ordinary had to occur for it to arise.

Naturally, you might assume that having the same tastes in sexual kinks would ensure sexual compatibility or at least overcome a huge hurdle to that, being that sexual incompatibility lists as a major and prevalent reason for broken relationships.

A recent study (de Jong & Reiss, 2014) proved that sexual compatibility isn't necessarily about liking the same kinks, though that obviously helps considerably. The study surveyed what kind of sexual activities each member of a couple liked, as well as how much they thought their partner enjoyed those activities. In other words, this survey would be able to determine how similar a couple's sexual preferences were and how complementary they were. Finally, they were surveyed about the amount of satisfaction they had with their sex life.

Surprisingly, similarity and sharing the same kinks was *not* the largest predictor of sexual satisfaction in a couple.

Instead, the only consistent predictor was how *complementary* the sexual preferences were for a couple. In other words, there is more sexual satisfaction to be had if one person likes being tied up and the other enjoys doing the tying—complementary—than if both people enjoy being tied up—similarity.

It seems obvious when you lay it out as such, but it's not so clear in practice. People categorize kink into large, general areas that don't accurately portray what someone actually enjoys sexually.

For example, if you show a sexual interest in feet, you might just want to worship someone else's feet but never have anyone touch yours. There is a distinct difference between the two. Sexual compatibility is about having complementary kinks, not similar ones, which means that you should seek out a partner who can give you what you want and vice versa, not necessarily a partner who wants exactly what you want.
Sometimes the two might overlap, and those are the most fortunate of circumstances.

Kink at some point should probably be downgraded into a mere sexual preference instead of evidence of a traumatic childhood. The science supports this in the way that some people like cilantro, while others can't stand it. Neither are defective, and both deserve to live their lives the way they want.

Engineer attraction and feelings of love through understanding how kinks work, and seek to complement others in bed to keep them coming back for more. What keeps us from exploring them more freely?

Perhaps you saw some porn that seemed really up your alley in all sorts of surprising ways. But none of that matters if you can't bring it up with your partner and have it done to you! Why are we afraid of approaching our partners, and why are we shy in a way that we normally wouldn't be?

Because we are afraid of them judging us. Rather than attempt to convince you away from this fear, I'll just say this: they've seen you naked and know what your orgasm face looks like. They've already judged you and are still having sex with you. They know that people like different things and that vanilla missionary sex isn't ideal for everyone.

If you're with a good partner, you won't be judged for wanting to try something new. They should actually encourage openness, expressiveness, and hearing your true feelings and preferences. And that should run both ways. Remind them that you aren't there to judge them and you might even want to reveal something vulnerable about yourself to set the open and nonjudgmental tone.

You can bring up the topic of kinks in two ways. The first is the direct way, and you already know it and want to avoid it. Therefore, the second method is a bit more incidental and spontaneous in nature. There is a big difference between, "Hey, sit down. We need to talk about something," versus a casual, "Hey, I just heard about this. What do you think?"

If you want to be slightly more indirect and feel safer doing this, you can concoct a story about the kink or spice that you want to introduce into your sex life.

"I just read about this kink . . . what do you think?" or "My friend just told me he did this . . . what do you think?"

That way, you aren't making a direct suggestion; you are simply bringing the topic up and gauging a reaction. When introducing your ideas, however you do it, the key is to not be aggressive or one hundred percent excited and forward about it. This might make them feel obligated to do it, even if they know they would hate it, if they see how strongly you want something. Don't push too hard, because then it will cause one party to be happy and the other party be to silent and resentful.

That's another reason why bringing it up spontaneously and not as a sit-down topic is better. Just put it out there and see how they feel about it without any pressure or expectation from you. The last thing you want your partner to feel is pressure or expectation. Create a safe space for them to talk about what they want and also turn down what they don't want.

If you're feeling bold, you can visit a sex shop for the same purpose. You are in the business of gauging reactions.

If all else fails, investigate using a website such as mojoupgrade.com, which lets you fill out kinks separately and only notifies you on what you match on. More importantly, it does not list the fetishes and kinks that only one person has listed. Therefore, it is a completely safe way to say what you want because they won't see what you've marked if they haven't also marked it.

After all, what good is exploration if you can't proverbially whip it out?

Takeaways:

- At this point in the book, you may have a better understanding of how to reach your goal of mating. However, in reality, your goal is sustained mating within a relationship. How can you make sure the sex is good enough to do that?
- Many sex tips focus on either specific techniques or exploring kinks to improve your sex life, but that's not what really matters. Studies have shown eight specific elements of great sex: presence, connection, intimacy, communication, authenticity, bliss, exploration, and vulnerability. This is empowering because it means literally everyone has the ability to be a great lover; it just takes time, energy, and attention.
- Exploring kinks, however, is never a bad thing. To do so, it's important to understand how a kink you come across,

including yours, may have arisen. There are typically five theories on the matter: adjacent brain theory, Pavlovian conditioning, pain, gross-out theory, and subjective normal theory.

- Yet, knowing your kinks and how they formed is of no use if you don't feel comfortable enough in bringing them up. You may find it easier to bring it up as a side topic purely to gauge reactions and create a safe space to talk about them.

Summary Guide

CHAPTER 1. ANIMAL ATTRACTION

- The classic sociobiological theory of attraction states that we are nothing but animals when it comes to attraction. Worse yet, most of what we are attracted to is subconscious and not fully understood.
- Waisman's four steps are an elaboration on the classic sociobiological theory of attraction. They inform us as to exactly what we are looking for in a way that fuses sociobiological theory with modern dating.
- The four attractions are physical, status, emotion, and logic. It is a sequence you must pass through for a deep and fulfilling relationship, although we know many that only satisfied two or three factors in their own relationships.
- The best way to use these four factors is to understand what phase you are in when you are evaluating someone and to understand where you may fall short.

- Human beings tend to want the same things in their mates—attractiveness, resources, and emotional connection—but people will rank the relative importance of these differently depending on their sex and their life stage. A good dating strategy takes this into account and finds a workable overlap.

CHAPTER 2. DON'T SAY A WORD

- Many animals don't have verbal languages. This means they must communicate their attraction, often forcefully, through their movements and actions. The human equivalent is how we communicate nonverbally with our body language, eye contact, and touching.
- There are different types of attractive body language for each gender. They do, however, depend on the factors of availability and fertility. Simply put, the more available you appear, the more attractive you will be, and the more fertile (this varies by gender) you appear, the more attractive you will be.

- When we think about trust, one of the first places our minds will go is to eye contact. Whatever the reality, if you aren't able to use eye contact, people will find you untrustworthy. Thus, eye contact has been found to cause people to attribute positive traits to you and see you as more intelligent and more trustworthy. But how do we wield eye contact without creeping people out or appearing untrustworthy? The thin line appears to be around three seconds of eye contact at a time, with sufficient rest between gazes.
- There have been found to be three types of touching in the context of flirting and attraction: friendly, plausible deniability, and nuclear. The most ideal mix is plausible deniability touching mixed with nuclear touching because of the message it sends and how it balances itself out. Friendly touching doesn't really factor into it, even though that's what we are most accustomed to.
- Playing hard to get is a proven tactic for increasing attraction, because it can increase your perceived value. Be careful about being mean or arrogant, though— you want to build pleasurable anticipation and expectation.
- You may appear more attractive when

people are unsure of your feelings for them, so don't be too transparent too early on. Give compliments, but let their meaning be ambiguous.

- Breaking rules can be attractive since it conveys confidence and power and communicates that you act from your own internal integrity, which is sexy! Never violate people's boundaries, however, and cause any actual harm.

CHAPTER 3. THE "CHASE"

- The chase is something we subconsciously do, despite outwardly decrying having to play dating games.
- Mostly, the chase has to do with the appeal and addictiveness of intermittent rewards and understanding why human nature works this way.
- The other portion of the chase is about how unavailability is attractive because we immediately begin to ruminate on what we are missing out on and what we are being deprived of.
- However, the chase is not a foolproof method, even though it takes advantage of

human psychology. Most of us have been faced with being rejected and told that we are only thought of as friends and not romantic partners. Is there a way to deal with this?

- For females, perhaps. Studies have shown that females do indeed see males platonically, but males do not do the same for females. Can males and females be only platonic friends? Yes, but it will usually be the female's choice.

- Finally, the deeper the love, the deeper the hate. Love and hate are closer than you think because they are both intense emotions. Work with love and hate in your own "chase" by leading with your polarizing attributes rather than aiming to please everyone in the boring middle.

CHAPTER 4. ALL ABOUT FLIRTING

- Flirting is hard to define, but in general, the goal is to gain someone's attention and make it known that you are interested in them. There are many ways to do this, but not everything will work for everyone.

- Researchers have additionally discovered

a three-step process people who were successful in leaving with someone from bars used consistently. The three steps are approach, synchronize, and touch. It's important to analyze what you are doing, what you are not doing, and if you are skipping over a step or staying on one too long. You should also consider how your flirting style fits into this process.

- This approach is best used in situations where you have reason to believe the other person is receptive to them.

- Dr. Jack Schafer's friendship formula states that people build connections when they are in proximity to one another, when their interactions are frequent and long in duration, and when both parties get their needs met.

- Schafer's theory can be applied to flirting, especially in contexts where the three-part flirting process wouldn't be appropriate.

- Whichever approach you use (short-term flirting or longer-term connection-building) remember top go step by step, building gradually on pervious connection, and adjust your approach carefully based on how you're being received.

CHAPTER 5. LOVE IS ALL THAT MATTERS ．

．．

- Love is what most of us marry for, but arranged marriages have been around for a very long time. In fact, what most of us would consider romantic love is a luxury that is only a few hundred years old.
- Arranged marriages work precisely because love is placed as a low priority. Instead, commitment, problem-solving, and lowered expectations take the forefront and create conditions that allow for a harmonious relationship to first blossom, which allows love to follow.
- Another factor that appears to be more important than love in relationships is similarity. Studies have shown that similarity is more important because people don't tend to change, and over time, you're just left with conflicting values and worldviews.
- The triangular theory of love states that the most successful relationships score well on all three metrics: attraction, intimacy, and commitment. Happy couples need to have strong overlap and match in their "triangles" or else work to

strengthen their weak points.

- A study specified the traits that predicted the most relationship success if similar: agreeableness and emotional stability. Conventional wisdom says that opposites attract, but for successful long-term partnerships, shared values and similarity in interest, communication, preferences, etc. are usually more valuable.

CHAPTER 6. HOW TO KNOW WHAT YOU WANT (YOU DON'T)

- We often think we know what we want based on singular experiences, stereotypes, or simple social pressures. But we are typically very, very wrong.
- In fact, most of the time, we are just making educated guesses. Psychological distance is deceptive, and we often confuse what we want with what benefits us from a self-interest standpoint. In reality, what we do know is simply what we don't want. This is not the same as wanting the opposite of what we don't want.
- Despite our own internal confusions,

there are certain scientifically proven traits we do seek in mates that are more related to biological imperatives. We are subconsciously drawn to excitement and arousal, fulfilling gender-specific arousal triggers, a sense of humor, and masculine and feminine voices.

- Research shows that while smiling and expressing happiness can make people like and trust you, when it comes to relationships and dating, this is not always the case: men find smiling, happy women most sexually attractive, but women tend to rate as more attractive those men who express pride (i.e., competence and self-assuredness) and shame (lowered gaze and awareness of social norms). At least initially, expressing happiness is theorized to convey a lack of status or dominance.

CHAPTER 7. ACTS OF THE AMOROUS NATURE

- At this point in the book, you may have a better understanding of how to reach your goal of mating. However, in reality, your goal is sustained mating within a relationship. How can you make sure the sex is good enough to do that?

- Many sex tips focus on either specific techniques or exploring kinks to improve your sex life, but that's not what really matters. Studies have shown eight specific elements of great sex: presence, connection, intimacy, communication, authenticity, bliss, exploration, and vulnerability. This is empowering because it means literally everyone has the ability to be a great lover; it just takes time, energy, and attention.

- Exploring kinks, however, is never a bad thing. To do so, it's important to understand how a kink you come across, including yours, may have arisen. There are typically five theories on the matter: adjacent brain theory, Pavlovian conditioning, pain, gross-out theory, and subjective normal theory.

- Yet, knowing your kinks and how they formed is of no use if you don't feel comfortable enough in bringing them up. You may find it easier to bring it up as a side topic purely to gauge reactions and create a safe space to talk about them.